THE FORMULA FOR
WEALTH

MY THOUGHTS ON WEALTH,
ENTREPRENEURSHIP AND LEADERSHIP

FEMI PEDRO

author HOUSE®

AuthorHouse™
1663 Liberty Drive
Bloomington, IN 47403
www.authorhouse.com
Phone: 1 (800) 839-8640

Published by AuthorHouse 04/16/2020

ISBN: 978-1-7283-5825-3 (sc)
ISBN: 978-1-7283-5823-9 (hc)
ISBN: 978-1-7283-5824-6 (e)

Library of Congress Control Number: 2020906210

Print information available on the last page.

This book is printed on acid-free paper.

The Formula for Wealth
My Thoughts and Experiences on
Wealth, Entrepreneurship, and Leadership

Femi Pedro

To everyone with an entrepreneurial spirit, and to anyone driven by the passion, commitment, determination, and will to create wealth.

CONTENTS

FOREWORD

The journey to wealth is a well-known mystery that can be discovered both deliberately and accidentally. Wealth is sought after by many, but only a few find true wealth in their lifetime. It is perceived to be elusive, but the path to it is well worn. Many have walked this journey; some find it by chance, and others search for it but never find it.

Femi Pedro's book joins many distinguished authors and writers, such as Dave Ramsey, Robert Kiyosaki, George Clason, Nimi Akinkugbe, and many other finance gurus in seeking to present the world with a visible and viable map, one that anyone on the quest to true wealth can use to guide them on this journey. There are timeless truths presented in his book. The wise would heed it, and the not so wise will miss it completely.

One of the challenges for millennials and Generation Z is combating the spirit of instant gratification in the pursuit of wealth. The way the media presents the "overnight" success of tech start-ups, the musicians and movie stars, athletes, and the sensation of reality TV and social media influencers hasn't done sufficient justice to the timeless truth that opportunity will always meet those who are prepared for it. Aside from gambling and the lottery, many "overnight" successes came from a lifetime of hard work, training, and preparation. Truly, some do get lucky and win big, but the reality is that luck cannot bring you wealth and, even more certainly, cannot keep you wealthy.

According to Femi, the first step on this journey is knowing the destination. He therefore distinguishes between wealth and riches. I like the way he puts it: money is liquid … it flows right through your fingers. Money in the bank (or under your mattress) is not true wealth. While the exact picture of wealth differs from person to person, it does look like financial security, financial independence, and financial freedom. For some people, wealth is in good health, a happy home, and contentment in what you have. For others, it is being a multibillionaire in US dollars. He leaves a lot of room for the reader to come to a comfortable position. A key essential in all these definitions is hard work. Femi is also clear that wealth will not derive from employment, leaving the seeker to just entrepreneurship.

A good education should make one functionally literate, able to not just survive but thrive in the world you find yourself, and teach the discipline of hard work and reward. If you study well, you get good grades, and the next level opens up to you. The real world may not be as linear as the academic environment in the hard work–reward cycle, but there is a reward for hard work. Wealth hardly embraces the indolent. While hard work is necessary, it is not sufficient. It is when hard work meets wisdom and a little bit of luck or divine favor that wealth is created. This is the only formula I know for the creation of wealth. The first two are in your direct control, and the third will always come to you if you have the first two. This is the mystery of wealth, the ability to recognize opportunity when it comes; but I believe everyone who works hard and applies wisdom gets their shot. If you cultivate the first two, you too will have your chance in the quest for wealth.

One thing that distinguishes this book from other finance and wealth books is its emphasis on entrepreneurship. Irrespective of which part of the world you live in, the journey to wealth is never easy. While the principles are simple, the path is difficult to navigate. Femi highlights the importance of developing one's entrepreneurial skills and acumen. Especially in the country context of Nigeria, the ability to fail quickly and learn, survive uncertainty and thrive are skills not just for discovering wealth but even attaining baseline financial security.

There are many stories shared that show that sometimes the issues we face are the result of environmental factors—especially political and economic. Our ability to handle these external issues and thrive despite adverse circumstances is determined by how well we have developed ourselves on the inside—in our minds—and also on our experiences.

This book contains a collection of wisdom both from experience and from others who have done their part to lay out the age-old principles of wealth creation and retention. Femi shares his personal experiences, those of others who have both succeeded and failed, as well as what he learned from the experts on the journey to attaining and retaining wealth. It is simple and worth reading to discover it for yourself. I believe he presents financial wisdom in an accessible and engaging way, as though one were sitting with him over lunch, asking him to share what he has learned on his journey to wealth. I believe this is a must-read for everyone from the age of eleven upward. After all, who would not want to discover the principles of living in true financial freedom?

It has been a personal privilege to write the foreword for Femi Pedro's book. Femi was a loyal member of the founding team of Guaranty Trust Bank. He was a good consensus builder, and as he transitioned to public service, he was considered a loyal deputy governor. I applaud his courage in telling his story of how he went from being the deputy governor under the Action Congress to the gubernatorial aspirant. He followed his ambition, and the essence of wisdom is being able to learn from our mistakes and present the authentic truth for others to learn from. Perhaps his greatest achievement, beyond attaining the measure of wealth he has, was in overcoming political adversity. Femi has restored his reputation and left an honorable legacy for his family. He has also been able to go back into the now All-Progressives Congress to continue to serve his state and nation.

As you read this book, for its wisdom to come to life, it must be applied. So, I want to encourage you to be an active reader. Start by formulating your own picture of wealth. Write it down. Paint a vivid picture. What does it look like? Feel like? Imagination is the tool that faith uses to bring the unseen into the seen. Describe it well enough, so that when you finally get there, you'll know it, because you've imagined it and seen it before. Build up good practices that you can follow diligently.

As you learn about the concepts of savings and investments, identify how you can start today. If you don't start, you'll never leave where you currently are. Be mindful of the people around you. It is easier to go far on a journey with others, so long as you're going in the same direction. Remember the formula: hard work plus wisdom meets opportunity.

Work hard and study the wisdom to be found here. As you go on this journey, may you also find it in yourself to give back. Supporting others both on the way and once you get there is part of the wisdom of retaining wealth. May divine favor meet you and catapult you in your journey to wealth.

—Fola Adeola, OFR; mni.

ACKNOWLEDGMENTS

Writing this book has been an extremely rewarding experience. As a first-time author, it has been challenging and exciting in equal measure. I would not have been able to write this book if not for certain people who played vital roles in the process.

I would like to express my sincerest appreciation to my wife, Jumoke, who sowed the seeds and convinced me to embark on this journey by chronicling my experiences. I was reluctant at the onset, but I could not be more grateful to her, because writing this book has been one of the most fruitful endeavours I have ever pursued in my adult life. I owe a debt of gratitude to my children—Bode, Biola, Bimbola, and Tokunbo—who all contributed immensely every step of the way.

A very special thank you to Deji Abodunde of Pierce Watershed Limited, who dedicated several weeks of his time to shaping my thoughts and words into a more compelling and engaging format. I am also immensely grateful to Fola Adeola, who was gracious enough to pen the foreword on extremely short notice.

Finally, special thanks to the folks at AuthorHouse Publishers, who carried the book over the line. This book would not have been complete without the professionalism and dedication they brought to the fore. Posterity will judge you all kindly.

ABSOLUTE
FINANCIAL
FREEDOM

FINANCIAL
INDEPENDENCE

FINANCIAL
SECURITY

GETTING
STARTED

POVERTY
TRAP

THE
WEALTH
LADDER

CHAPTER 1

Winners Don't Quit

You just can't beat the person who won't give up.
—Babe Ruth

It always seems impossible until it's done.
—Nelson Mandela

It was in the late 1990s. Nnamdi Ezeigbo, an electrical engineer in his late twenties, had just failed to secure his dream job of working in a multinational oil company. It was disappointing, but he was determined to press on. He thereafter approached a friend who ran a computer repair shop in Lagos to learn about the business. From here—with meager start-up capital—he began an incredible journey that would lead to the creation of one of Nigeria's most successful technology brands.

Not long after, Ezeigbo parted ways with the friend. As he recollected years later, "My partner and others around me were only interested in making as much money as they could and had no scruples ripping off customers. I was uncomfortable with this practice and was told that I was 'spoiling business' and could not continue with them." Afterward, he opened his own repair outfit and operated it out of one corner of a bookshop.

FEMI PEDRO

Word about his credibility and competence soon spread around the Ikeja area. He became known as the guy who would fix your computer at a reasonable cost and deliver on time. As a result, his clientele grew rapidly.

With the opportunities and funds that came from the increased business, he branched into selling computer parts. He began making trips to Dubai to buy parts, which he sold to retailers and repair shops in Lagos. Soon, the bookshop corner became too small for his operations.

About this time, he got a break. He made a huge profit from selling a consignment of printers that had been given to him by a customer. With this, he was able to lease a large office space and put up a huge signboard that said, "SLOT LTD."

The business experienced growth for a while but then got stuck; he just couldn't get it to grow any further. As would later become clear to him, this was because of fundamental problems. First, the company was being run without any clear vision, plan, or governance structure. Second, many of the employees were family members whom he hired because he believed he could trust them. Finally, he lacked the knowledge and skill to make the structural transition from a sole proprietorship to a corporate enterprise.

Ezeigbo knew something was not right, but he couldn't discern what it was. On the advice of a friend, he decided to go back to school to learn more about business management. He enrolled at the Lagos Business School's part-time MBA program. "I was enthralled by the new knowledge and the brainstorming sessions. It was like my business was dissected and a surgical procedure conducted," says Ezeigbo. "The experience was akin to a blind man seeing for the first time."

Fresh out of the MBA program, Ezeigbo began to restructure and reposition his business. He replaced redundant employees—many of them family members—with experts. He hired a consulting firm to set up a comprehensive financial, operational, and corporate governance system, and a board of directors was also constituted. Before long, the reorganization began to bear fruit. The business expanded rapidly, and new shops were opened in Lagos and Abuja.

When the Global System for Mobile Communications (GSM) was introduced into Nigeria in 2001, SLOT was well positioned to make massive profits from the new technology. MTN, the leading Nigerian telecommunication company at the time, approached him to allocate space in his shops to sell their SIM and recharge cards. The gains were huge. First, traffic in his shops exploded. Second, MTN paid rent for the space. Third, he got a commission on every SIM and recharge card sold.

Shortly thereafter, MTN expanded into mobile phones, with the introduction of the Nokia 3310—with a locked SIM—into the Nigerian market. While MTN's mobile phone business was booming, Ezeigbo observed that customers were unhappy that the phones were locked and concluded that this was an opportunity.

On one of his trips to Dubai to buy computer parts, he stumbled on the unlocked version of the phone. He decided to test the waters and brought back a shipment. He sold each phone at half the price of MTN's locked version. Customers were thrilled, and his entire stock sold out in a matter of days. This began his transition from the computer parts and repair business to the mobile phone business.

Ezeigbo soon spotted another opportunity when he noticed that many Nigerians had to carry multiple phones because of the patchy service of the GSM operators. At the time, the telecom companies had more subscribers than their installed capacity could handle, and service quality dropped. This period also marked the beginning of the smartphone era, with Samsung and Apple as the market leaders. Many Nigerians—young people in particular—desired to own smartphones, but the offerings from Samsung and Apple were unaffordable for most people.

Ezeigbo and his team began to explore solutions. He met with a Chinese company and convinced them to partner with SLOT to develop a smartphone that would carry two SIMs. The dual SIM phone concept had not gained traction anywhere in the world, and the company considered it a huge risk to design and manufacture a phone with the Nigerian market primarily in mind.

But he convinced them that the Nigerian market was big enough to justify the investment. This led to the birth of TECNO and, later, Infinix products. The TECNO phones initially introduced into the Nigerian market were poorly designed, and customers were reluctant to buy. SLOT lost a lot of money at this stage and was only able to sell off its stock through aggressive marketing.

Determined to succeed despite the setback, Ezeigbo and his team went back to the drawing board and came up with a sleeker and more functional phone. This was a game changer. TECNO had now emerged as an alternative smartphone to Samsung and Apple products.

Despite the tough environment, Nnamdi Ezeigbo has created wealth beyond his wildest dreams. He is now widely recognized as one of the most successful entrepreneurs in Nigeria and controls a business empire that is worth millions of dollars. Today, SLOT operates in more than six hundred shops nationwide, and the company has expanded into selling computers and electronics as well as entrepreneurship training.

Ezeigbo's story captures the essence of this book. My purpose for writing is to help millions of young people who are disillusioned or frustrated or just need guidance and encouragement. I am passionate about sharing my experience, in as much as it can help other people, and I believe that the ideas and stories in this book will be helpful to young people who want to make a success of their lives in Nigeria and other developing countries. Our youth are smart and energetic, and given the opportunity, they will move mountains.

What were the factors responsible for Ezeigbo's success? The first is *integrity*. When others around him were ripping off their customers, he resisted the temptation, even though it would have brought him a lot of profit. Second, his *resilience*. Building a successful business requires a large dose of tenacity. Many of life's failures are people who did not realize how close they were to success when they gave up. Third, his quest for *knowledge*. He took the bold step of enrolling for an MBA during a period when his business was demanding a lot of his time. He also attended the owner/president management program at the Harvard Business School. Fourth, his *financial discipline*. When Ezeigbo's business really began to take off, he resisted the urge to build houses, buy exotic cars, and acquire other luxuries. He chose to put much of the new cash back into the business instead. Finally, his ability to continually *innovate*. According to him, the MBA program broadened his thinking and sharpened his creative skills.

Like Ezeigbo, around the world are thousands of wealthy and successful entrepreneurs whose stories can inspire Nigerians, especially the youth, in their quest to be successful and prosperous. These entrepreneurs span every corner of the globe. Their stories prove that wealth creation is universal and cuts across geographical, racial, religious, cultural, and gender barriers. I hope that the knowledge gained from this book will encourage you to believe that your situation is not hopeless, and I hope this book will inspire you to act to change it.

Importantly, you do not have to be a billionaire, or even a millionaire, to be considered successful. The simple criterion is that you own investments (in businesses, assets, and other wealth instruments) and your net worth generates enough income that can sustain you for a long time without having to work for money. In other words, your money works for you. With this, you can afford the basic needs of life without ever having to struggle again.

It is my firm belief that this goal is within the reach of millions of Nigerians, if they apply the principles discussed in this book. Wealth creation is a matter of choice and commitment. Rich people are *committed* to being rich. Poor people *want* to be rich. What is keeping you from being wealthy? In most cases, it is simply a lack of belief. In order to become wealthy, you must believe you can do it, and you must take the actions necessary to achieve your goal.

What qualifies me to write this book is the broad knowledge and experience I have gained while serving in both the public and private sectors for more than four decades. Also, I have had extensive and close relationships with some of the wealthiest people in the world and have observed their lifestyles. I have also read countless books on wealth creation and learned valuable lessons that I have practiced in my own life. I have drawn on these to develop a blueprint for wealth creation.

Some of the stories and principles I share are from the books that have had the greatest influence on my journey. These include *The Richest Man in Babylon* by George Clason; *More Important Than Money*, *Rich Dad, Poor Dad* and *Cashflow Quadrant* by Robert Kiyosaki; and *Money: Master the Game* by Tony Robbins. Others are Ramit Sethi's *I Will Teach You to Be Rich*; Steve Mariotti's *The Young Entrepreneur's Guide to Starting & Running a Business*; T. Harv Eker's *Secrets of the Millionaire Mind*; and Andreas Pira's *Homeless to Billionaire*.

The next chapters are devoted to defining wealth and poverty and analyzing the major reasons why only a few people end up attaining the financial freedom that everyone craves. The subsequent chapter explains the difference between *just* making money and *actually* creating wealth. There, you will see that it is possible to make money, even lots of it, but still end up being poor!

The next chapter deals with what I believe are the foundational principles of wealth creation: a positive mind-set, your habits and thoughts, dreaming big dreams, finding your passion, having a mentor, financial discipline, and keeping the right company, among others. This chapter is followed by the fundamentals of entrepreneurship and a simple guide to best practices in managing a successful business. Next is the chapter on investing in equity and real estate. The final chapter focuses on the leadership lessons I have learned over the course of my career as both a corporate executive and a politician.

I have been privileged—personally and professionally—to have had some really great experiences. I have been fortunate enough to have met amazing people who inspired me to make the right choices, set proper goals, invest in the right businesses, and, in the process, create significant wealth. Now, I want to inspire others to do greater and bigger things with their lives. I want to motivate you to change your thinking and lifestyle, so you can create a better future for yourself.

The general tendency is to allow the sociopolitical and economic situation in Nigeria to dampen your spirit and discourage you from doing amazing things. Every day, the news is filled with stories about corruption, terrorism, crime, poverty, university strikes, and failed businesses. This can affect your thoughts and actions, creating negative emotions and energy. You must program your subconscious through positive thinking. You must adopt the mind-set of wealthy people, who are usually determined to succeed against *all* odds. You must live by the principles of honesty and integrity. You must be resourceful, innovative, passionate, and visionary. You must learn how to think big and dream big. Getting started can be overwhelming, but you must make up your mind to succeed.

I strongly recommend this book to everyone who desires a prosperous life, particularly young people between the ages of twenty and thirty-five. There is no age limit to wealth creation, but I believe the young generation will find these principles easier to adopt and apply.

CHAPTER 2

Wealth Means Freedom

It's not how much money you make, but how much money you keep, how hard it works for you, and how many generations you keep it for.

—Robert Kiyosaki

I have about concluded that wealth is a state of mind, and that anyone can acquire a wealthy state of mind by thinking rich thoughts.

—Edward Young

Wealth is defined as the state of being rich or materially prosperous. It is synonymous with affluence, well-being, and luxury. Wealth produces a feeling of empowerment, security, and being in control of one's destiny. It makes people feel alive and in charge. Wealth—or the absence of poverty, which is a state or condition in which a person lacks the financial resources and essentials for a minimum standard of living—is one of the most fundamental aspects of human freedom.

Wealth means different things to different people. For some, it means a quiet and comfortable life, free from any worries. For others, it is an opportunity to touch lives and make an impact on society: think of Bill Gates and his globally influential foundation.

For most people though, wealth is simply an opportunity to live a purposeful life. Nothing beats being able to afford anything you need or want; travel anywhere you wish without worrying about the costs; and being able to support the people or causes you are passionate about.

Most people desire to be wealthy and live a purposeful life, but only a few are ever able to achieve this. A major reason for this is ignorance about wealth creation. Creating wealth is a methodical, deliberate, and intense process: it requires knowledge, purpose, tenacity, determination, and patience.

The true measure of wealth is your net worth measured by the total value of wealth instruments you own. Wealth instruments can be in the form of real estate, quoted equities, bonds, private shares, private ownership of business, rare gems, rare artworks, and anything of value that can be traded or sold in the open market anywhere in the world. Wealth instruments have a more enduring value than money.

Real wealth is the income generated from wealth instruments. If you own a wealth instrument such as real estate, your wealth is the rent you receive or the proceeds from its sale. Likewise, if you own equities, your wealth comes from the dividends and capital appreciation. If you own a business enterprise, your wealth is the profit you generate from the business.

Owning an expensive house, exotic car, or costly furniture does *not* necessarily make you wealthy. These assets do not generate income. They simply add to your expenses due to maintenance and insurance.

If a person comes into a large sum of money—by winning the lottery, through inheritance, or through some other windfall gain—the person is rich in cash but *not* wealthy. He or she can simply be described as someone with a lot of money. Such people soon realize that money is liquid. If uninvested or handled recklessly, money loses its value or completely vanishes over time.

How can you determine if a person is wealthy? A person is wealthy if they have substantial ownership of any of the following—business enterprises, equities, bonds, real estate, savings deposits, rare gems and stones, antiques and artworks—to a point where these instruments generate enough income to provide *financial security, financial independence,* and *absolute financial freedom* for life.

Financial security is the ability to take care of the basic needs of life without stress. This includes ownership of a home fully paid for; comfortable transportation with the ability to replace or upgrade regularly; and enough funds to cover food, utilities, clothing, medical, and educational expenses.

Financial independence is having not only enough to guarantee your financial security but also much more to pay for luxuries such as vacations, the latest electronic gadgets, and expensive cars, without having to work for it. It means you have everything you need (and want) today, and the means to sustain this for the rest of your life.

Absolute financial freedom is to have financial independence and much more to be able to set up a foundation, give to charity, and donate to social and political causes. It means you can afford to do anything you want at any time you want to do it. It means you can afford to make a monumental difference in other people's lives or even change the course of history.

The minimum required for anyone who desires a decent life of happiness, good health, and general well-being is *financial security.* Both financial independence and absolute financial freedom are a bonus.

Do you have financial security? What net worth will yield an annual income that you consider enough to make you financially secure? This varies relative to an individual's taste, family size, and age. Your target depends on what you want in life. Some people are fine with basic *financial security,* while others want to achieve *absolute financial freedom.*

Whether you aspire to be as wealthy as Bill Gates or Aliko Dangote, or you are content with simply being able to meet certain basic needs for the rest of your life, it is important that you are not struggling financially or reliant on a salary as your only source of income, and that your investments are working for you and not the other way around. It is important that you can do without working for a long period and still live comfortably.

Unfortunately, only a few people are able to achieve this level of financial security in their lifetime, while the majority struggle through life. Why is it that only a few people are extremely wealthy, and a large proportion are poor? What are the factors that distinguish a struggling cobbler from the billionaire owner of a shoemaking empire? What separates the founders of Uber from the struggling taxi driver? How did people like Steve Jobs, Oprah Winfrey, Richard Branson, Mark Zuckerberg, Bill Gates, Aliko Dangote, and Mike Adenuga create products and services that have made them billionaires?

These questions will be answered in this book, but it is important to state that the success stories of these entrepreneurs show that you too can do it. Do you wish to be wealthy and successful? Are you ready for a life of prosperity, happiness, and peace of mind? If the answer is yes, then you can start your journey to great prosperity today.

Contrary to popular belief, you do not have to belong to a wealthy or popular family to become wealthy. Neither do you have to be connected to some godfather or be related to someone in government. Let me also assure you that you do not need a university degree or a professional qualification to become successful. You also do not have to be supremely intelligent or talented. Indeed, a large percentage of people who are struggling financially or trapped in poverty are talented professionals and well-educated people.

THE
TRUE FACE
OF POVERTY

CHAPTER 3

The True Face of Poverty

Poverty entails fear, and stress, and sometimes depression; it means a thousand petty humiliations and hardships. Climbing out of poverty by your own efforts, that is something on which to pride yourself, but poverty itself is romanticized only by fools.

—J. K. Rowling

If you are born poor it's not your mistake, but if you die poor, it's your mistake.

—Bill Gates

Poverty is defined as the state of being poor. It is synonymous with penury, pennilessness, impoverishment, indigence, and lack. Just like wealth, there are varying degrees of poverty, ranging from extreme poverty to moderate poverty. Anyone who struggles financially and constantly lacks the means to meet their needs and wants is trapped in one form of poverty or the other. The majority of people are stuck somewhere between moderate and extreme poverty and, despite their best efforts, cannot get out of this condition. The state of being perpetually poor and not being able to find a way out of it is known as the "poverty trap."

Most people have a strong desire to be wealthy but never achieve financial independence and wealth in their lifetime. Many well-educated and hardworking people with good careers still end up struggling financially: they are typically in the middle class but sadly never attain any significant measure of wealth. It is often a mystery to them as to why they are in this quagmire.

Some have spent their entire lives working in public service in middle- to senior-management positions, or in the private sector, earning a decent salary. A significant number run their own businesses or professional consultancies yet struggle financially throughout their working years and eventually retire into *penury*.

All the categories of people I have just described are stuck in a poverty trap. This situation is one of helplessness and of perpetual financial strain. It is akin to finding oneself in a deep well with a blindfold on. It is very difficult to find a way out, because you cannot see a solution even if it is right in front of you!

This situation is even more acute among young people who are still in their prime. They are still fresh, idealistic, energetic, and ambitious but are jobless with no useful skills, and they lack the basic knowledge of the elements of wealth creation. This ultimately leads to frustration, anger, helplessness, and hopelessness. This condition drives many to channel their energies in the wrong direction.

When people struggle financially, they become disorganized and confused and lose confidence in themselves. As a result, they develop a poverty mentality. They play the role of the victim and blame everyone but themselves for their situation. They blame the economy, the government, their employer, their chosen business or profession, their parents, their marriages, and even the devil!

There are millions of Nigerians who are extremely poor and whose situation seems hopeless. Many of them can improve their condition if they are empowered through training, capacity building, and skill enhancement so that they can become gainfully employed or self-employed. Indeed, there are many empowerment programs instituted by governments at all levels, private sector organizations, and several nongovernmental and charity organizations designed to pull people out of extreme poverty.

These measures, though laudable, are clearly not adequate to cater to the millions of people who fall into this category. Our fast-growing population has compounded the problem: most children born into poverty are likely to remain stuck in it as adults and are likely to perpetuate the vicious cycle through their offspring. A major cause is the poor education infrastructure across the country, which results in a high illiteracy rate.

Education—in its numerous varieties—is a major key to poverty eradication and financial independence. It is only through education that you acquire the knowledge and competence to be creative and productive. It is difficult for an illiterate farmer to learn modern methods of farming and improve his crop yield; the same goes for an illiterate micro-entrepreneur, who will find it nearly impossible to identify new sources of funding, understand new business practices, and access new technologies. Improving the literacy rate by enforcing laws on universal primary education will go a long way in bridging this gap.

Having said that, there are millions of educated people who live in poverty because they are financially illiterate. They struggle to make ends meet and have to use all their income to pay for rent, taxes, feeding, health care, and other basic needs, thus leaving little to nothing for emergencies, savings, or any form of investment.

Many people rely solely on a monthly salary and are constantly in fear of losing their jobs. They are heavily dependent on securing salary increases, medical benefits, salary advances, and short loans. There are millions of others who run micro and small businesses and struggle to earn a meager income that is often inadequate to sustain themselves and their families. Many retirees earn a meager pension and have to depend on others to survive. Significantly, there are millions who simply cannot find any job.

Many people find good jobs after getting a higher education and settle down to what they hope will be a life of comfort. Unfortunately, they soon find themselves struggling, and this persists for most of their adult lives. Their education has given them new skills, professional aptitude in highly technical areas, and knowledge about many real-life tasks but has not taught them how to create, grow, and retain wealth. They may be smart and hardworking, but if they lack the aptitude for wealth creation, they will be trapped in poverty.

I was once in this category. I grew up in a poor and struggling family: my parents and grandparents were trapped in a cycle of poverty. About a year after I was born, my mother became pregnant again, and her health deteriorated. In the search for better medical attention, she relocated to Minna (Niger State), where she stayed with her elder sister, whose husband (my uncle) worked with the Nigerian Railway at the time.

At the age of two, I was sent to live with my paternal grandmother—Mama Ajah Sabalemot Abebi Pedro—at Ajagun court, Lagos Island. Mama Ajah had been widowed for about ten years prior to my birth and was in her early sixties at the time. She was extremely poor and solely relied on the allowance she received from her children, including my father. The allowance was meager and irregular, but that was what we lived on for many years.

We lived in the hallway of the main living room in the family house. A single bed was placed in a corner for my grandmother, and I slept on a raffia mat by her bedside. This was my home for ten years until 1967, when I completed primary school.

I was not really aware of the extent of our poverty at the time, because everyone who lived around us was also very poor. I saw my situation as normal. Fortunately, the Western Region government introduced free and compulsory education, and as a beneficiary of this policy, I enrolled in a primary school near our home in 1960. The only things I worried about were school uniforms and books.

For my secondary education, I went to a boarding school in the Agege area of Lagos. This was the first time I truly grasped the extent of my family's poverty. My secondary school years were a constant struggle between studying and getting good grades and paying my tuition and boarding fees. After my tuition and boarding fees had been paid—jointly contributed by my maternal grandmother and my father—there was almost nothing left for my upkeep.

My secondary school was a mix of children from rich and middle-class families and those from poor homes. The visible lifestyle of the kids from well-to-do families served as a constant reminder to the less fortunate kids that we were poor! They came to school with boxes full of food items, clothing, and cash, and they used these items to buy privileges from seniors and house masters, while the poor kids were treated with scorn and made to do all the hard labor.

Deeply troubled by my situation, I approached one of my favorite teachers and asked him what I needed to do to escape poverty as an adult. He simply said, "Face your studies, pass your exams, gain admission to the university, and the rest would fall into place." I was sixteen years old and in the fourth form and took his advice hook, line, and sinker.

I became more motivated and focused than ever, and I studied tirelessly to obtain good grades in the final year exam, to enable me to secure a place in the higher school for A-levels, which was the surest path to university admission at the time. I eventually gained admission to university and graduated with a degree in economics and decided to pursue a master's degree in the same discipline.

Unfortunately, I did not realize quickly enough that a university degree merely gave me a good education in a discipline but did not guarantee a noticeable pathway out of poverty. I was a graduate, but I was still a financial illiterate. My teacher was not wrong in encouraging me to get a higher education, but he had not shown we how to *escape* the poverty trap!

In 1982, right after my National Youth Service, I landed a dream job at the Central Bank of Nigeria. My immediate career goal was simply to rise through the ranks until I attained a senior management position. My assumption was that by climbing the corporate ladder and earning a good salary, I would automatically become a wealthy person.

But after six years and two promotions, along with a corresponding salary increment, I realized I was not really attaining the success I had imagined, neither was I happy with my job. In that period, I became a husband, and then a father, and then a father again and again! I had very little to show for my years of hard work in terms of wealth and assets. All my earnings, which were decent relative to the standards at the time, were devoted to meeting personal needs and raising my young family.

I did not own any real estate, any stocks or bond, or any form of assets. I was unable to set anything aside to acquire wealth instruments because every penny went into meeting my daily living expenses. I was struggling financially, but I did not understand why. Instinctively, I knew that something was missing, but I was not sure what it was. Critically, I *knew* I was in some sort of trap, and I was determined to get out. The silver lining was that I was happily married to an equally hardworking and intelligent wife, Jumoke Pedro. She was—and still is—a dutiful, caring, loving, and charming wife and mother to my children.

At this early part of my adult married life, Jumoke was a practicing lawyer and subsequently a magistrate, before she became a high court judge. We were both salary earners. In spite of our combined monthly income, we were struggling financially. Our financial situation was worrisome to me, and I began to wonder how we could ever attain a level of financial security.

This became even more obvious whenever I observed my boss. He was a fifty-five-year-old assistant director and was a few years away from retirement. He joined the bank right out of university, had worked there for more than thirty years, and had risen through the ranks to become a senior manager. Despite all this, I could see that he was clearly still struggling financially.

He owned a home, thanks to a thirty-year mortgage from the bank. But his salary—after tax and other deductions—was so little that it was barely enough to meet his family's needs. He owned no wealth instruments, and his whole life depended on only one source of income—his monthly pay. His situation was pathetic; he was always under serious financial pressure.

As a young banker, I learned a lot of things from my boss, but I was unimpressed by his lifestyle, his shabby dressing, and his continual complaints about his financial situation. I soon realized that the odds favored me ending up like him (or even worse) if I stayed at that job for too long.

At that point, I began to look for a better-paying job. I had the erroneous belief that more money would simply make me richer, happier, and more fulfilled. I assumed that with a higher-paying job, I would have more money and therefore more wealth.

I eventually resigned from the Central Bank and got a new job with a private bank. My new job came with a higher pay, better perks, and allowances, and it was more glamorous. I was very proud of it and showed off my new status to my friends and colleagues. My lifestyle changed for the better, reflecting my new position: I bought a car with a loan from my new employer, joined the prestigious Ikoyi Club with my family, enrolled my children in the school of our choice, and acquired a new set of trendy suits, shoes, and fashion accessories.

I worked harder than ever before, spending countless hours at work and fewer with my family, but I earned more than I ever did. However, my expenses continued to rise to unimaginable levels, and I soon realized that despite my higher earnings, I was not better off than I was in my old job. Although I was earning more money, I was also *spending* more.

Still, I gave no serious thought to savings or investment. I was in no hurry to play the capital market big-time, as I assumed that only the superrich bought shares. My whole life revolved around *working*, *earning*, and *spending*. Nothing for a rainy day. I did not know it then, but I was still deeply rooted in the poverty trap. If I had lost my job by some stroke of bad luck, I would have been in serious trouble.

The reality is that there is very little correlation between academic success and wealth creation. It bears repeating that many intelligent university graduates are financial illiterates. The following case studies are real-life examples. For obvious reasons, their real names are not disclosed.

John: Smart, Hardworking, but Poor

John, a mechanical engineer, graduated with a second-class upper degree from the University of Lagos. He got a dream job with a leading construction company immediately after his National Youth Service. His starting salary was decent, and shortly after getting the job, he rented a flat in a suburb of Lagos close to his office. He applied for a loan from his office to pay for the three-year rent his landlord demanded. Later, he took another loan to pay for his wedding expenses.

John was promoted three times over a ten-year period; he was a middle manager by the time he was forty and was now earning four times his starting salary. But at forty and married with three children, he still struggled financially and lived from paycheck to paycheck.

Multiple loans made him so heavily indebted to his employer that he could not even contemplate a change of job. He did not own a house, had no investment of any kind, and had not been able to maintain any form of savings. His expenses had grown way beyond his income, and he could hardly keep up. When he eventually realized that he was trapped in poverty, he had no idea on what to do to improve his situation.

I know his story because I was his landlord for a few years. We became good friends, and I decided to mentor him after listening to his story. He is presently following my blueprint for wealth creation and is determined to see a turnaround in his life.

Henry: Brilliant Doctor with Zero Business Acumen

Henry ran a private hospital in Lagos in the early 2000s and operated an account with First Atlantic Bank at the time I was the CEO. He once got a three-year loan from the bank and defaulted on interest and principal just one year into the repayment schedule. The bank got a debt collector to pursue the recovery and sell-off of the collateral security—his property—which served as both the hospital and his private residence. It was during this crisis that I met Henry. He was frustrated, disillusioned, and scared. He pleaded with the bank to grant him some concession and more time. After listening to his story, I felt very sorry for him, and I was determined to help him out of his predicament.

Henry graduated top of his class at the College of Medicine, University of Ibadan. After a few years of working at a private hospital in Ibadan, he moved to Lagos to open his own hospital. The initial capital came from loans from his parents, other family members, and a friend. With the money, he rented and renovated a twin duplex. One wing was the clinic, and the other was his private accommodation.

The hospital saw a lot of patients during its first five years but could not break even because most of them were poor and could not afford the consultation fee. He tried to make up for the paltry fees by working long hours so he could attend to more patients. The hospital also suffered because some patients took advantage of Henry's generosity, leaving the hospital with unpaid medical bills that they never returned to settle.

In the sixth year of the business, the landlord decided to sell the property and gave Henry the right of first offer. Considering that he had spent a lot of money to renovate the property to suit his needs, he thought it wise to buy it. That turned out to be a major mistake.

Desperate to buy the property, he approached my bank, pledged the property as collateral, and took a loan of forty million naira. He added ten million naira from his savings and purchased the property. In applying for the loan, his accountant prepared an audit of the hospital's account for the first five years and a projection for the next five years, which showed a profitable enterprise.

Unknown to the bank, the accountant had presented a falsified audit report and an exaggerated projection, which painted a rosy but false picture. Unfortunately, the bank's due diligence was too weak to detect the misrepresentation at the time, and the loan was granted.

Reality soon set in. Henry's troubles started when his actual revenue fell far below the accountant's projection, and he struggled to service the loan. He started defaulting on the interest from the third month, and after a six-month moratorium, on the principal.

Upon close examination of his situation, I realized Henry was an excellent doctor but a poor and inexperienced entrepreneur. He was brilliant at his medical practice but did not have adequate training in entrepreneurship and business management. He granted too many credits and had a poor accounting structure. In addition, his employees frequently stole money and pilfered the hospital's equipment.

More importantly, he should not have bought the property at the time, because his cash flow could not support the loan repayment. To make things worse, his accountant padded his books, making it look better than it was. As a result, he was on the verge of a foreclosure and risked losing everything.

After several weeks of going back and forth, we put the foreclosure on hold and advised him to make some changes. First, he fired his accountant and engaged a more professional firm. Second, we advised him to sell the property while he remained a tenant and continued to run the hospital within the premises. Fortunately, we found a buyer who paid a fair price that covered the loan and accrued interest. Third, we hired a consulting firm to restructure his business. The consultant advised him to hire a business manager to handle the business side of the hospital, while he focused on the medical practice. His system was optimized to improve efficiency in service delivery. Finally, upon our recommendation, Henry agreed to enroll at the Lagos Business School to improve his business and entrepreneurship skills.

Henry's hospital survived the crisis and is a thriving business today. He is forever grateful for the bank's intervention in saving him from potential calamity.

Bala: Underemployed and Angry Banker

Bala graduated from the Tafawa Balewa University, Bauchi, with a bachelor's degree in agricultural science but had no interest in pursuing a career in agriculture. He wanted to work in a bank, so he moved to Lagos to stay with his uncle—a ram trader. He got a job as a contract staff with a bank and had worked there for more than five years when I met him.

One day, I engaged him in a conversation while at the bank, and then he blurted out his frustration. As a result, I set up a meeting with him to discuss what he was going through. He explained to me that his monthly salary was ₦80,000 after tax, half of which was spent on transportation, feeding, and rent. He was angry and felt unfulfilled, because he worked long hours, spent a lot of time commuting to and from work, and had little or nothing left at the end of the month.

It was obvious he had no plan for his future and did not exactly know what he wanted from life. I started having a weekly mentoring session with him. During this period, I realized that he had been helping his uncle with his accounting and, in the process, had acquired valuable knowledge about the ram business. I advised him to take a leave from work so he could devote more time to learn about the business.

He informed me at the end of the month that he was quitting his job, because he saw good prospects in the ram business. Unknown to him, he had discovered his passion. Again, I advised him to continue with his job at the bank for six more months, during which period he could save up a third of his income to be used as start-up capital. It would also give him time to further understand the business.

Bala did as advised and subsequently became a ram and livestock entrepreneur. Today, he travels to the north once a month and brings back a trailer load of ram, goat, and guinea fowl to sell in Lagos. Drawing from his banking experience and information technology skills, he created a website and payment platform through which he sells livestock to customers. He tripled his turnover within a few months and is presently a thriving entrepreneur and no longer angry and frustrated.

Chief Aluko: Astute Politician and Failed Entrepreneur

Chief Aluko was a popular businessman. He landed huge contracts from which he earned a substantial profit. He became a big spender, built a large mansion, and bought expensive cars. He married a second wife and sent two children to study abroad.

Our paths crossed from time to time for several years. I studied him and could see he was a poor man who had a lot of money. *He had money but was not wealthy.* Unfortunately, I could not help him before his financial bubble burst. The juicy contracts subsequently dried up, and he was left out in the cold.

Despite his situation, he could not adjust to fit the new reality. He persisted in his wasteful lifestyle. Two years later, he contested for political office and lost. This was the last straw because he exhausted all his savings on his political misfortune. Chief Aluko was left with a mansion and a fleet of cars he could not maintain, two wives and numerous children who were already accustomed to an expensive lifestyle, and a failing political career.

When I visited him in 2010, his condition was pitiable. He had suffered a mild stroke, and his health was failing. He had sold all his cars, and one of his wives had abandoned him. His friends and political associates had also deserted him. He was full of regrets, and it was too late to help him. He died a couple of years later.

The examples discussed above illustrate what many people go through in their quest for financial security. The four of them desired to be wealthy, or at least to become financially secure. Bala and Henry were fortunate to have discovered the right path on time and subsequently changed course. On the other hand, Chief Aluko's story ended tragically.

The Poverty Trap

Due to the poor economic situation, many Nigerians desperate for survival look for quick fixes to their financial predicament. Exploitative, get-rich-quick schemes have flourished as a result, further impoverishing people and sometimes ruining their lives. A get-rich-quick scheme is one that promises to make a person wealthy within a short period, often with little effort and at no risk.

Many of these schemes have perfected the art of hoodwinking desperate people who desire to be wealthy but do not have the knowledge, mind-set, and patience required for legitimate wealth creation. A very common get-rich-quick scheme is the Ponzi or pyramid scheme, in which participants are recruited to make payments and enroll others, with a promise of higher future income without any form of investment instruments. In the last few years, many people have lost their money and much more to Ponzi schemes. Despite this, many continue to take part in it out of desperation. These schemes are illusory and fraudulent, and the operators only exploit the ignorance, greed, and desperation of those in the poor and low-income bracket of society. They ask you to contribute an amount and promise extraordinary returns within a short time. They collect contributions from several others and use this cash to settle claims from earlier contributors as they become due. The operators of the scheme do not invest their funds but manage it for profit; they merely transfer funds from one client to another. They simply build it up for as long as they can sustain it before it crashes. Like all pyramids, when it is stacked too high and for too long, it will come crashing down. Most participants end up losing their money. The best way to identify these fraudulent schemes is that they always promise fantastic and mind-boggling returns on investment. You should be wary once the promised return is far more attractive than conventional financial market returns. Second, the operators are usually not licensed financial institutions; they operate illegally or exploit a legal loophole to stay in business. Third, the operators usually do not have any verifiable track record in the financial sector. Ponzi schemes should always be avoided.

Another get-rich-quick practice is gambling. Gambling is the practice of wagering money on an event of uncertain outcome, with the primary intent of winning more money. There are many forms of legal and illegal gambling schemes, such as casino gambling, sports betting, lottery games, and poker. All are addictive and are neither a healthy nor viable way of creating wealth. Studies have shown that gambling can become addictive and harmful. Addiction to gambling can have negative effects similar to drug and alcohol addiction. Gambling operators use marketing gimmicks to hoodwink players, sometimes even giving them a line of credit, but it invariably leads to financial ruin. Once a person is addicted, they will borrow, steal, and do just about anything to get more money to gamble with.

It is rare to find someone who became wealthy through any form of gambling. In contrast, the world is littered with stories of ruined lives and failed marriages as a result of it. Young people are particularly vulnerable, because the operators target their marketing at them. In recent times, an alarmingly high number of young people—primarily out of desperation but also out of frustration—have taken to this addictive habit. Some people actually engage in full-time gambling; they play the lottery or mobile sports betting week in, week out, hoping to hit the jackpot and become overnight millionaires. However, the odds of winning the jackpot are incredibly slim, and most people end up being poorer. The few who get lucky and win large sums often lose all or most of it within a short time.

Another trend among young people, especially well-educated and accomplished professionals, is to emigrate out of the country because of the perceived lack of opportunities to grow and prosper in Nigeria. It is believed that better opportunities exist in developed economies, and the chances of succeeding are higher. The reality is that wherever you are in the world, the fundamental principles of wealth creation hold true. While there is nothing wrong with seeking greener pastures in other countries, many people do so without a cohesive plan, thereby setting themselves up for a lifetime of struggle and frustration. Migration in itself is not necessarily the solution to a life of financial struggle, and moving to another country comes with its own set of complexities. Relocation must be purposeful and vision driven. Relocating to acquire new skills, new knowledge, and more experience or to take advantage of greater opportunities in advanced economies is highly encouraged. Migration out of frustration and desperation may lead to wasting productive years by having to take on menial jobs.

Perhaps, the most intriguing trend among young and unemployed persons is to dabble in politics, with the primary aim of becoming wealthy. In truth, the most successful politicians are the ones who have previously built successful businesses or careers prior to their sojourn into politics. Young people who choose the path of full-time politics with no entrepreneurial or professional pedigree usually end up at the lowest rung of the political ladder. A lot of people are attracted to politics due to the perceived displays of wealth by politicians and people with connections to the powers that be. Dabbling in politics for this purpose mostly ends in frustration and failure. Only a few people who pursue political office simply for monetary gain actually succeed. They eventually lose most or all of their money to bad investments, wasteful spending, and political misadventures.

THE
MONEY
ILLUSION

CHAPTER 4

The Money Illusion

Money is a tool. Used properly it makes something
beautiful; used wrong, it makes a mess!
— Bradley Vinson

If you wish to get rich, save what you get. A fool can
earn money; but it takes a wise man to save and dispose
of it to his own advantage.
— Brigham Young

The lack of knowledge about wealth creation has caused many
hardworking and talented people to mismanage their affairs and plunge
deeper into the poverty trap. As noted earlier, talent, intelligence, a
great job, or even a good salary do not by themselves guarantee financial
security if you do not understand the principles of wealth creation.

I have known many people who started well by securing good jobs
and climbing the corporate ladder, yet they become financially stranded
at some later point in life. It is not because they became lazy or less
ambitious but because they did not adequately plan for their financial
future. The following case study is a real-life example, but for obvious
reasons, their real names are not disclosed.

A Tale of Four Friends

John and Remi were among my top-performing managers when I was CEO of First Atlantic Bank; their results were always exemplary, and I was very proud of them. Both were flamboyant and ambitious. Dapo was soft-spoken and simple: he mostly kept to himself but was very hardworking and reliable. Mike was equally hardworking and productive. The four of them were good friends and often hung out together.

The four friends—all in their late thirties—were at a bar one evening when John and Remi began to brag about their overseas vacations, exotic cars, trendy suits, fancy gadgets, luxury wristwatches, and other belongings. They went on and on. Meanwhile, Dapo said very little.

"What do you do with your fat salary and bonuses, dude?" Dapo was asked.

He responded calmly, "I am careful about my spending. I save and invest to ensure I am prepared for the future no matter what happens to this bank or our industry."

His answer puzzled his friends. Why would he be talking about an uncertain future on a lovely evening and at a time when they were having the best period of their careers? Unfazed by their reaction, Dapo continued: "Have you guys thought of what would happen to you and your exotic cars, fancy suits, and all the luxuries of life if this bank goes bust?"

They were uncomfortable with this line of discussion and quickly dismissed his pessimism. One of them teasingly called him "Baba Ijebu" (a miserly person). They joked that he needed to learn how to enjoy life more.

As Remi recollected, "John and I felt we were living the good life. Our salaries, bonuses, and allowances ran into millions. We enjoyed our jobs. Even though it came with some pressure and stress, the pay was good. Within a few years, John had built a block of apartments in the city. I purchased some quoted shares, went on family vacations abroad, and bought a brand-new car for my wife. Mike was spending lavishly on his wife and his extended family. He opened a gift shop for his wife along Allen Avenue, which cost a lot of money. He rebuilt his family home in his hometown and was responsible for sponsoring his younger brothers in the university.

"Dapo's lifestyle was modest. He lived in a rented apartment and drove an old Toyota Camry when the rest of us were using SUVs. He never took vacations outside the country; he preferred to visit his town or travel within the country. We often made fun of him and always reminded him to enjoy life. He never told us what he did with his money, and whenever we asked, his response was always the same: 'You cannot predict the future; it is wise to prepare for the future by being prudent today.'"

Around this time, John took another loan from the bank, mortgaged his block of flats, and built himself a new house. Remi kept buying new cars and globe-trotting. Mike continued to spend on his wife's shop, his family home, and other luxuries.

Then in late 2004, Charles Soludo, the governor of the Central Bank of Nigeria, announced a recapitalization policy that shook the banking industry and resulted in drastic and far-reaching changes. Out of eighty-nine banks, only eleven were sufficiently capitalized. Within a few months, fourteen banks were suddenly wound up, and the rest were advised to merge. Only twenty-five banks emerged from the consolidation exercise. One of the twenty-five was Finbank Plc, formed from the consolidation of First Atlantic and three other banks.

Many people were caught napping by the development; jobs were lost and careers ruined. The four friends were fortunate to survive the massive layoffs, but their careers suffered. "Finbank was not the same as First Atlantic Bank, and the culture and business practice changed," Remi recalled. Bedeviled by boardroom squabbles, distrust in the management, and unending infighting, Finbank itself did not survive for long and was acquired by First City Monument Bank.

By 2012, all four friends had lost their jobs amid the endless mergers and acquisitions. The future that Dapo foretold was now a reality. John was the first to exit the bank. He tried to join another bank but was unsuccessful. After a year of chasing nonexistent jobs, he gave up. He began to live on the rent from his property—about ₦6 million per annum. This was a far cry from the twelve million naira (salary, allowances, and bonuses) he had been earning from the bank annually.

But he chose to not adjust his lifestyle. He kept his children in expensive schools, and his wife continued to drive the high-maintenance SUV. Eventually, he could no longer service the loan he took to build his house. By 2014, the bank foreclosed the block of flats he had mortgaged to acquire the loan. His life was in shambles.

Mike and Remi were retrenched immediately when Finbank was acquired. Mike got another job as a manager in a microfinance bank, but the new job paid far less and was not as glamorous as the previous one. Within a year, he was fired because he could not meet his target. He could not afford to pay the rent due for his wife's shop, and they were subsequently kicked out. Frustration and resentment eventually cost him his marriage.

After Remi lost his job, he put together his savings, shares, and severance pay—about ₦10 million—and decided to start a business. A friend sold him on the idea of starting a fish farm. He took him to a fish farm at the outskirts of Lagos, whose owner boasted about the fantastic returns and profitability of the venture. He decided to embark on the business without any knowledge of fish farming and without a business plan. "I had the mentality of a banker and not an entrepreneur," he recollected. "I started big and pumped all my cash into the business, leased a large plot, and built different tanks with a total capacity for ten thousand fish. I employed local boys as my handlers to keep and feed the fish. But after a few months, I realized it was not the same as my banking job; it was a high-risk business that required a hands-on approach. I could not afford to take my eyes off it, even for a minute."

But this realization came too late. Over time, the boys gradually sold off the fish whenever he closed at night. His harvest was barely 10 percent of his projections. It was a disaster. The business collapsed within a year.

Dapo saw what was coming much earlier than his friends. He left the bank a few months before the others were laid off and immediately traveled to China to meet with a software company looking for a reliable Nigerian partner to market their financial services software.

Once they decided to go ahead, Dapo used all his savings and investment as security deposit for the partnership. He spent six months in China with the parent company to study the products and marketing techniques to enable him to handle the Nigerian operation. The partnership worked out well, and the business grew rapidly; it expanded to other West African countries, including Ghana, Cote d' Ivoire, and Senegal. Dapo is now the group managing director for Africa.

Remi continued the story. "After leaving the bank in 2012, we all disappeared into our new lives. In 2015, I was desperately looking for contracts here and there to keep body and soul together, when I was given a note to see the managing director of a software company, hoping to supply stationeries. I was ushered into his tastefully furnished office, only to see Dapo as the managing director!

"Dapo had transformed his life completely. The reunion was a mixture of sadness and joy. We compared notes. John had been bedridden for a while, having suffered a stroke. He had a mental breakdown after he lost his house, was forced to sell all his cars, and had to pull his children out of the expensive schools. Mike moved back to the east when he could no longer cope in Lagos. He got another job as a manager of a microfinance bank in Enugu and had also divorced his wife. Here I was, sitting in the sprawling office of my friend and former colleague, the one we often derided as 'Baba Ijebu.' He is now my benefactor."

The story above is typical of many people who are mesmerized by money yet lack the knowledge required to create wealth. These were four professionals, well educated, hardworking, and productive. They got to a point in their lives when they had enviable jobs and fantastic salaries, but they lacked purpose and vision. They lived only for the moment and expected their fortunate circumstances to last forever. Dapo was the only one who had a clear financial blueprint and lived wisely. The others did not, and as a result, a sudden change of circumstance destabilized them and sent their lives in a downward spiral. I mentored Remi and encouraged him to refocus his career. I told him all was not lost and that he would be able to turn his life around, provided he was willing to learn from his mistakes. Remi decided to embark on a new career in real estate, and I encouraged him to get a job where he could learn the ropes from accomplished professionals. Today, Remi is a qualified real estate professional and manages a real estate company. He is full of excitement and hope for the future.

The main lesson here is that money is an illusion. Money is liquid. It comes and goes, and it is unprotected. The majority of people struggle financially because our thoughts are shaped by the long-held maxim that says, "If you work hard, someday, you will be rich." A lot of people cling to the illusion of job security and see their monthly paycheck as their means of escaping poverty.

More importantly, at the start of their careers, these men did not understand the fundamental principles of wealth creation, entrepreneurship, and investing. They had poor personal financial-planning habits and did not prepare for the rainy day. It is imperative for everyone to continuously attend seminars on entrepreneurship and wealth creation in order to be prepared for life beyond today.

Professional athletes, high-profile entertainers, lottery winners, and those who suddenly come into a large inheritance are particularly prone to the money illusion. If you belong to this group, then you should pay attention, because you have a unique set of challenges.

The foundational principles of wealth creation require a step-by-step process through which you become more knowledgeable, more appreciative, and more experienced about growing and sustaining wealth. A person who becomes wealthy by practicing these principles is unlikely to make poor financial decisions that could lead to losing it all very quickly. On the other hand, many professional athletes, entertainers, and lottery winners come by money without necessarily going through this process. In technical terms, they have a lot of money but are not wealthy. They are rich, but they have not built enduring wealth.

Having a lot of money is not synonymous with being wealthy. Money is liquid and can evaporate, whereas wealth is solid, stable, and growable. Money cannot be preserved or grown. Money will lose value over time, unless it is wisely and skillfully invested and managed for growth and multiplication. It is only then that money *becomes* wealth. The world is littered with examples of professional athletes, entertainers, and everyday people who suddenly came into large sums of money and soon lost it all due to mismanagement and ignorance. They became vulnerable to the shenanigans of con artists of all varieties—hangers-on, crooks masquerading as financial experts, duplicitous tax lawyers—all of whom are equipped with all sorts of mechanisms to rid the unsuspecting of their money. The tragic financial stories of many world-renowned athletes are painful to recount. A few examples are worth noting. "Athletes have a different set of challenges from, say, entertainers," says money manager Michael Seymour. "There is a far shorter peak earnings period [in sports] than in any other profession, and in many cases, they lack the time and desire to understand and monitor their investments."

In the 1980s, Mike Tyson was a young and successful boxer. He was one of the most recognizable names in the world of sports. During this period, "Iron Mike," as he was dubbed, earned about $400 million, raking in an average of $30 million per fight at the peak of his career. Sadly, while he was making all that money, he also engaged in destructive financial behavior. He spent lavishly on jewelry, mansions, expensive cars, parties, expensive clothing, and even Siberian tigers. He became heavily indebted and filed for bankruptcy. Tyson became rich and famous very quickly but was ignorant of the principles of wealth creation.

Michael Vick was a gifted and talented American NFL football professional. He earned nearly $40 million per year at the peak of his career but lost it all within a few years. Vick lost his fortune to reckless spending on family members and associates, gambling, lawsuits, and a conviction for engaging in dog-fighting activities. Vick's poor choices, recklessness, and financial naïveté enabled his agent to fleece him of millions.

Artists are another vulnerable species when it comes to money management. The rapper 50 Cent, a talented and successful entertainer, started his career in the crime-ridden ghettos of New York. He sold more than thirty million albums and won dozens of awards at the peak of his career. At some point, he was the second richest hip-hop artist in America. However, a background of poverty, coupled with inexperience in handling money, led him to invest poorly, while spending in an unsustainable way. Unlike many others in this category, 50 Cent invested part of his earnings in wealth instruments, even though some of his choices were poor.

High-earning professional athletes and entertainers tend to venture into entrepreneurship without adequate preparation. Venturing into financial investments while active in sports can be risky and distracting, and many lose fortunes in the process. There is the case of Curt

Schilling, a baseball professional who invested in a video game company and filed for bankruptcy after racking up more than $150 million in debt against assets that were worth less than $21 million. Dulymus McAllister, an NFL footballer, made tens of millions of dollars during his career. While still playing, he invested some of his money in a Nissan car dealership, which went bankrupt shortly after he defaulted on his payments and exceeded his credit line. By the time he retired, he had already lost much of his earnings, defaulted on his mortgage, and was rendered penniless. Mark Brunell was a successful baseball player who was worth more than $100 million at some point. He squandered his money on nine failed business ventures. Houston Rockets' Ismail Abdelmoneim earned more than $18 million in salary. He made several reckless investments—in a religious movie, a music label, and in a theme restaurant, among others—and lost all his money.

The list of athletes who earned a lot of money and lost it all to failed business ventures or reckless spending is endless: Vin Baker (basketball); William Perry (American football); Debi Thomas (ice skating); Kenny Anderson (basketball); Arantxa Sánchez Vicario (lawn tennis); Denis Rodman (basketball); O. J. Simpson (football and acting); Dorothy Hamill (figure skating); John Daly (golf); Boris Becker (tennis). Records show that 78 percent of former NFL players have gone bankrupt or are under serious financial stress. An estimated 60 percent of NBA players end up being broke within five years of retirement. Accomplished athletes are highly proficient at what they do but often lack the knowledge, passion, resilience, and patience required to manage their money. They easily fall prey to the machinations of desperate people who pose as financial advisers, tax experts, investment specialists, protective family members, and concerned friends. Many of these sorry tales would have been avoided if they imbibed the rudimentary stages of wealth creation and financial independence.

The first step is self-education. Entrepreneur and author Jim Rohn observed: "Formal education will make you a living; self-education will make you a fortune." Many renowned athletes and artistes have college degrees or have attained a decent literacy level, have above-average intelligence, and are mentally strong. It is therefore relatively easy for them to learn about personal money management on their own, while still active in their careers. One way to do this is by reading books and journals and attending seminars.

The second step is to hire a reputable firm with a track record of successful wealth management. Such firms employ experts in the areas of investment, trust management, legal advice, tax management, cash management, and insurance. These services are important for professional athletes and artists and enables them focus on excelling at their careers while growing and multiplying their wealth. These firms will create a budget, analyze cash flow, plan charitable giving, and establish an emergency fund. They will advise and help with proper tax planning, mortgage financing, private banking, portfolio choices, investment management, life and disability insurance, estate planning, and vetting of legal agreements. Athletes and artists are more vulnerable to signing unvetted agreements, thus ending up with costly lawsuits. The presence of a reputable firm serves as a deterrent to con artists, phony advisers, and other predators.

The third step relates to retirement planning. Most professional athletes retire young. American NFL and NBA players retire below forty on the average. The same is true of European soccer players, track-and-field professionals, boxers, wrestlers, and tennis players. Their earning years are short, and they have longer years of retirement, meaning they need to plan properly. The best approach is to start retirement planning as early as five years before the intended date.

As will be seen in the fundamental principles of wealth creation, if the retiring athlete desires to become an entrepreneur, he or she should start by finding their passion, submitting to the wisdom of a mentor, and acquiring knowledge in that area. These steps are important before a retired athlete ventures into any business.

There are many cases of successful athletes who managed their transition properly and became successful entrepreneurs. One example is Alex Rodriguez, a celebrated and accomplished baseball player and one of the greatest sportsmen in recent history. While still playing professionally, he made investments in real estate that turned out to be very profitable. He began with the acquisition of a single duplex and soon graduated to major real estate deals. Later, his company diversified into industries spanning sports, wellness, media, and entertainment.

The company has now grown into a fully integrated investment firm serving as investment advisers to other notable athletes and entertainers with assets worth billions of dollars, far exceeding Rodriguez's net worth at retirement.

Justin Forsett—a nine-year professional NFL player—is another athlete who made a successful transition to entrepreneurship. While playing professional football, he and former college mates—Wendell Hunter and Wale Forrester—developed a solution to a problem they had encountered as football players in the university. They realized that after many sweat-drenched workouts, they hardly had time to shower, which resulted in hygiene-related problems. They also found out that this was the case with thousands of athletes around the country. As a result, they developed an antibacterial, disposable body wipe, ShowerPill, which became an instant success.

Michael Jordan, arguably the most successful professional basketball player in history, has been successful on and off the basketball court. Jordan owns an NBA franchise—the Charlotte Hornets—and enjoys lucrative endorsement deals with Gatorade, Hines, and Upper Deck. He also has a lucrative sportswear partnership with Nike, where his special brand, Air Jordan, is so popular among African Americans that it grosses more than $1 billion in sales annually.

Jay-Z, the richest black entertainer in the world, with a net worth of more than $1 billion, has successfully combined entertainment with entrepreneurship, thus amassing a large fortune over a relatively short period of time. He has earned millions in sell-out tours and albums, but much of his wealth comes from entertainment labels, a designer clothing line, a music-streaming service, and exotic alcohol brands.

Shaquille O'Neal has also made a successful transition from professional basketball to entrepreneurship. O'Neal realized that he was financially illiterate when he was a basketball star. He appointed professional money managers to handle his affairs and maintained rigorous discipline in handling his money. He earned close to $300 million during his basketball career but has doubled that amount as an entrepreneur. His business interests span a restaurant franchise, endorsement deals, gyms, nightclubs, real estate, and a substantial equity in Google.

DREAMS & DETERMINATION	CHARACTER & INTEGRITY	PERSONAL FINANCIAL DISCIPLINE	CULTURE OF SAVINGS

POSITIVE WEALTH MINDSET	THE RULES OF WEALTH			FIND A PASSION

DEVELOP A BUSINESS IDEA & CREATE YOUR PATH	BECOME AN APPRENTICE	FIND A MENTOR	KEEP THE RIGHT COMPANY

THE
RULES
OF WEALTH

CHAPTER 5

The Rules of Wealth

Before you can become a millionaire, you must learn to think like one. You must learn how to motivate yourself to counter fear with courage.

—Thomas J. Stanley

Wealth is largely the result of habit.

—John Jacob Astor

Those who achieve great wealth do certain things differently from others. Wealth creation does not come as a result of luck or fate and is not entirely a product of education, intelligence, or hard work. The great majority of successful businessmen and women have been strong personalities of the right sort, and by analyzing their climb to success, it is amazing to discover how large a part good manners, good breeding, and correct behavior have helped them to attain the goal.

Wealth creation requires the application of certain fundamental principles, and based on these principles, I have developed a set of rules of wealth that are the blueprint for wealth creation.

A Positive Wealth Mind-Set

Most successful people think in a certain way. A study of the lives of those who feature regularly on the Forbes list of the world's richest people reveals a recognizable thinking pattern. This mind-set, usually created during their formative years, fundamentally shapes their emotional and social stability, as well as their overall outlook on life. Many people desire to be wealthy but cannot understand why only a few attain it. If a person's mind-set is not structured for wealth creation, then there is little they can do that will make much difference. Warren Buffett once remarked, "I always knew I was going to be rich. I don't think I ever doubted it for a minute."

Factors such as upbringing and general habits condition many people to be risk averse, unambitious, or overly dependent on others for their success in life. The subconscious minds of many have been negatively preprogrammed by their upbringing. This has in turn shaped their views about money. Many people will be familiar with the following statements, some or all of which were drummed into them while growing up:

- Money is the root of all evil.
- Rich people are greedy and corrupt.
- Money does not grow on trees.
- You must work for money.
- The rich get richer, and the poor get poorer.
- Money does not buy happiness.
- Work is the antidote for poverty (from the Yoruba saying, "*Ise l'ogunise*").

These words have shaped our understanding and ideas about work, money, and wealth. If you were raised by parents who harped on the importance of studying hard and getting good grades in order to be gainfully employed in the civil service upon graduation, then it is likely that you have been conditioned to see your future success as dependent on a government job. Your ambition in life would inevitably revolve around this.

The other aspect has to do with the financial situation in your family while you were growing up. A person who grows up in a household that constantly lacked basic needs, or where anger, fear, arguments, and frustration over money matters was the norm, most likely has a mind-set about money shaped by these factors. As a result, this person is more likely to have imbibed wrong ideas about money, which then manifests in the following ways: a tendency to play it safe with money; constant anxiety about poverty; an unhealthy deference to wealthy people; contentment with mediocrity; fear of change; and a complete reliance on hope and prayer for prosperity.

If you have been wired to have a negative view about money and you do not change it, you are likely to be stuck in a life of penury.

It must be your goal to change your mind-set about money. American philosopher and psychologist William James noted, "If you can change your mind, you can change your life." According to former British prime minister Benjamin Disraeli, "Nurture your mind with great thoughts, for you will never go any higher than you think."

It is also possible to be raised in a family where positive values about wealth and entrepreneurship are encouraged through words and actions. One of my childhood friends, Akeem, was raised by parents who were both entrepreneurs. His mother was a fabric trader, and his father a building contractor. Akeem never lacked money and was very generous to his friends.

During the holidays, Akeem would go around hawking designer clothes and wristwatches. I confronted him when I thought he was hawking stolen goods. He took me to the marina quay area in Lagos, where he bought clothes and jewelry from sailors who came with ocean liners. He bought at cheap prices, because the sailors needed quick cash to send to their families before their vessels sailed again. I watched in awe as he negotiated like an adult and brought out wads of cash to pay the sailors. He made a handsome profit from the sale of the items. I was curious about how he got into the business. His mother encouraged him to go into the business by loaning him the initial capital with which he started trading. For a sixteen-year-old, Akeem's entrepreneurial acumen was extremely impressive.

One day, Akeem offered me a bag of clothes as a gift. My suspicious grandmother questioned Akeem about the source of the clothes. Refusing to accept his explanation, she insisted that I return the clothes and warned me to never associate with him again. As far as she was concerned, Akeem was a thief.

Today, Akeem is a very successful real estate investor. He imbibed an entrepreneurial mind-set from his parents at an early age and grew up with the outlook of a billionaire. My grandmother, on the other hand, could not accept that a young man of Akeem's age could trade in expensive clothing unless he was a thief. She instilled this mind-set in me, and it ended up being a big hindrance on my path to wealth creation.

This situation is typical of many households. This is not because the parents do not mean well. They simply have a wrong notion about money and wealth. It is important to spend time reviewing your own history regarding how money was modeled to you as a child, as well as the emotional experiences that you can associate with it. Invariably, you will discover that your present mind-set was most likely shaped by these experiences.

The good news is that you can still change your money mind-set. The first step is to become conscious of the fact that you have imbibed thoughts and beliefs that are hindering your ability to create wealth. The next step is to be determined to discard these ideas. A billionaire believes they can create the kind of life they desire, while a person trapped in poverty simply believes life just happens, and they have no control over it.

It is easy to blame others for your situation. It is much more productive to search your past and find what caused your faults. When you blame others, you give up your power to change. This feeling of control or lack thereof is fundamental to why many people struggle financially. People play the victim and blame others for their financial predicament because they feel powerless about their situation. The blame game never works, because it does not change your circumstances. It only compounds it. If you desire wealth, you must think positively and believe that your destiny is in your own hands.

I have always been fascinated by the story of Mark Cuban, the son of Russian immigrants who fled the former Soviet Union to escape the persecution of Russian Jews. Cuban developed a positive financial mind-set early in life. At twelve years old, he sold garbage bags to buy a pair of shoes. At sixteen, he took advantage of the *Pittsburgh Post-Gazette* strike and began getting newspapers from Cleveland to sell in Pittsburgh—a distance of about 160 kilometers. His ability to sight a potential opportunity and capitalize on it to create wealth marked him out early as a successful entrepreneur. He paid his way through college by taking up odd jobs as a bartender, a disk jockey, and a salesman for a software company. He developed his business ideas and honed his entrepreneurial skills during this period. He formed a chain of companies that eventually became very successful. One of them was sold to Yahoo for nearly $6 billion. He has amassed a fortune through his companies and successful investments and is now worth more than $4 billion.

Mark Cuban's story highlights the need for a positive mind-set—a determination to succeed irrespective of your circumstances in life. David O. McKay noted, "Your thoughts are the architects of your destiny." Abraham Lincoln also said, "Always bear in mind that your own resolution to succeed is more important than any other." Cuban did not sit in a corner complaining about his lot in life. He took responsibility for his future. He was willing to work several jobs to see himself through school and was innovative enough to seize the opportunity that the *Pittsburgh Post-Gazette* strike offered.

Dreams and Determination

One important trait of wealthy people is their commitment and determination to be wealthy. B. C. Forbes, a financial journalist and founder of *Forbes* magazine, once said, "The men who have done big things are those who were not afraid to attempt big things, and who were not afraid to risk failure in order to gain success."

Imagine a twenty-year-old college student who repeatedly tells his friends about his ambition to be very wealthy within ten years. He might be labeled as overambitious, but this is the kind of mind-set that is equipped to create wealth. Author and educator William

Arthur Ward noted, "You must eliminate small thinking! Nothing limits achievement like small thinking; nothing expands possibilities like unleashed imagination."

There is a difference between someone who is casual about their desire to be rich and a person who is committed to becoming rich, and whose thoughts, actions, and behavior reflect this reality. If you want to become wealthy, you must learn to dream big, think big, be adventurous, be a risk-taker, and have a can-do attitude. Massive success comes from extraordinary discipline, dedication, and the power of big thinking. You must have and execute large ideas.

Successful entrepreneurs are creative thinkers who challenge the status quo and are willing to push the limits of what has been previously considered impossible. In the process, they come up with ideas and products that change the world. If you are not doing some things that are crazy, then you are doing the wrong things. You have to train your mind to believe the impossible can be achieved.

Whenever an impossible idea comes to your mind, do not immediately dismiss it as impossible. Write it down in a journal and ponder over it. It is possible to create or develop unlimited opportunities in your business through this process. As Christopher Reeve observed, "So many of our dreams at first seem impossible, then they seem improbable, and then, when we summon the will, they soon become inevitable." Think about the Wright brothers!

People struggle in business because they start out of desperation and the need for survival. They had no dream, no articulated vision, and therefore no direction. In other cases, the problem is one of narrowmindedness. Many people do not believe they can ever grow to be big, so they limit themselves to their comfort zone. For example, if you are into retailing, you may choose to be a retailer in a corner shop, or you can aim to become the next Amazon or Jumia or Alibaba. Wealth creation requires vision and determination!

The story of Otunba Subomi Balogun, one of Africa's most successful entrepreneurs, illustrates the power of dreams and determination. In 1978, at the age of forty-four, Balogun resigned from his job as an executive director at ICON Stockbrokers to set up his own company, City Securities Ltd. The odds were stacked against him at the onset, but his vision and determination made him carry on. Like other graduates of the time, Balogun grew up with the dream of becoming a top executive in a financial institution. Trained as a lawyer, he started his career at the Nigerian Industrial Bank and subsequently moved to ICON Stockbrokers, where he gained vital managerial experience in investment banking and stockbroking. This was where his interest in entrepreneurship and his dream about founding a bank began.

He seized the moment during the Nigerian Indigenisation Decree of 1978—which mandated foreign companies operating in Nigeria to divest between 40 and 60 percent of their holdings to indigenous investors. Realizing that the sale of these enterprises—many of which were top-tier Nigerian companies in the oil and gas, manufacturing, and financial-services sectors—would be handled by investment and stockbroking firms, he decided to set up his own outfit. This was his first venture into entrepreneurship. He faced so many obstacles, including the struggle to raise the initial capital to set up the company, but he persevered. After the company commenced operation, he struggled to compete with well-established firms to win lucrative mandates. His dexterity, zeal, and determination eventually paid off when he landed the issuing house mandate of the Nigerian Bottling Company. City Securities became very successful, and within a few years, Otunba Balogun was daring enough to apply for a banking license. Getting the license was not an easy feat because of the various structural, institutional, and political bottlenecks. But after about three years of relentless effort, it was granted. When the bank—First City Merchant Bank—was established, it was the first Nigerian bank in the modern era to be wholly owned by Nigerian investors.

I was fortunate to join the bank in 1988 as an assistant manager. I was immediately captivated by the corporate setup and ambience. It was very different from the working environment at the Central Bank of Nigeria. A few days after resumption, I had a one-on-one meeting with the entrepreneurship guru himself. This was a man I had read a lot about and watched on television.

Here I was in the presence of greatness. I was nervous and tongue-tied for a few minutes, but I eventually regained composure and answered his questions. Despite my nervousness, I must have made a positive impression on him because I was made his executive assistant almost immediately.

It was in this position that I was able to observe him closely and where I saw firsthand some of the habits that lead to greatness. First was the culture of excellence that defined everything that Otunba Balogun did. There was an elegance to his leadership, his communication style, and his dress sense. Everything around him had the stamp of excellence. He expected everyone in the bank to imbibe the culture of excellence in the work environment, customer service, and communication. I saw his doggedness and determination as he negotiated deal after deal. Working with him was a transformative experience for me.

The wealthiest Nigerian entrepreneur alive is Aliko Dangote. He has achieved tremendous success primarily because of his unique ability to thrive under unfavorable macroeconomic conditions and compete with global conglomerates. Dangote has proven himself to be a tenacious, focused, and determined entrepreneur. As a staff of First City Merchant Bank in the late 1980s, and later at Guaranty Trust Bank in the 1990s, I was able to observe him as he competed with the Indians and Lebanese in the importation of rice and sugar. I observed as he survived adverse government policies regarding foreign exchange, import license, interest rate, import duty, and even an outright ban on importation. Many of the local companies who ventured into this business could not handle the pressure and eventually collapsed. Not only did Dangote survive, he thrived.

Character and Integrity

Most people who have built significant wealth are people of integrity and strong character. They place a premium on transparency, trustworthiness, reliability, and faithfulness. You cannot succeed in the very competitive world of business if you lack these values. According to Warren Buffett, "You are looking for three things, generally, in a person: intelligence, energy, and integrity. And if they do not have the last one, do not bother with the first two."

Integrity simply means honesty and moral uprightness in whatever you do. It is at the core of every successful business relationship and makes it easy for people to rely on other people's words and actions. Most people take this for granted and pay a huge price for it. You cannot be successful if people do not believe that your word is your bond. Albert Einstein noted, "Whoever is careless with the truth in small matters cannot be trusted with important matters."

Author and speaker Zig Ziglar remarked, "The foundation stones for a balanced success are honesty, character, integrity, faith, love, and loyalty." Some people believe that you cannot make headway in business without telling lies. The adage "honesty is the best policy" still holds true today. You may be able to achieve some measure of success without these values, but it will eventually come crashing down. Mary Kay Ash wrote, "Honesty is the cornerstone of all success. Without honesty, confidence and ability to perform shall cease to exist." It is common to see people with shady pasts masquerading as successful entrepreneurs. Some of them are well-known swindlers. They may have money, but they are not wealthy. Their success is temporary and unsustainable. According to the book of Proverbs, "Wealth from get-rich-quick schemes quickly disappears; wealth from hard work grows over time."

I saw integrity modeled during my time at Guaranty Trust Bank. The bank was unique because these values were not merely stated on paper but were adhered to, promoted, and rewarded. The bank came into existence during a period when many new banks were licensed, and the operating environment was extremely competitive. The industry was crowded with many desperate and aggressive banks competing against the more established banks that controlled more than 70 percent of the market. The new banks needed to gain market share if they were to survive, and in the process, they resorted to underhanded deals, including "brokerage commission," to secure big accounts. Many of them encouraged their employees to engage in malpractices in order to stay competitive. These practices were unsustainable, and eventually many of these banks collapsed. Between 1989 and 1999, more than sixty Nigerian banks collapsed. People lost their jobs, careers were ruined, and some went to jail. This happened because primarily due to greed, mismanagement, and dishonesty.

Guaranty Trust Bank was among the few that survived the chaos. From inception, the bank made it a policy not to pay any form of commission to third parties, offer bribes, or engage in any unethical practices to gain new customers or attract deposits. This policy was consistently emphasized at induction programs and at every monthly performance meeting. The bank's stated values were strictly followed by the board, the executive leadership, and all cadres of staff.

In 1994, the leadership of the bank introduced the staff to Stephen Covey's materials—especially his book, *The 7 Habits of Highly Effective People*—and encouraged us to study and adopt them in our personal lives and work. I have found them to be some of the most important resources on integrity that I have ever come across. I was so enthralled by Covey's teachings, which deal extensively with building personal ethics and a principle-centered life, that I read and reread the book and regularly listened to his audio recordings. According to Stephen Covey, "The quality of our thoughts determines our actions and our actions develop our habit. Our habits create our character and our character forges our destiny."

We lived and breathed these values. There were no sacred cows; the few who violated this policy were instantly dismissed. Because of the strict enforcement of this policy, the bank relied solely on its products, service offerings, and aggressive marketing to compete. During the early years, it was difficult to secure the business of the major corporations and multinationals. But through hard work, persistence, and staying true to our core values, the public soon recognized the bank's strong corporate governance and principles, and it was rewarded with an avalanche of customers, individual and corporate.

Most importantly, these values were personified by the management of the bank, led by Fola Adeola, who demonstrated moral authority and exemplified the bank's culture. He was a great leader. He treated employees respectfully and showed concern for their personal well-being. He fostered a work environment where communication was open, transparent, and effective. He promoted a culture where excellence was visibly and instantly rewarded.

Fola Adeola walked his talk, and the staff not only respected him but desired to emulate him. He valued integrity, transparency, responsibility, and loyalty. We never had cause to doubt his stance on honesty and integrity. This, in turn, gave his team the confidence to always do the right thing, even in very difficult circumstances.

In 1993, I was appointed the head of corporate services—overseeing the administrative, human resources, legal, and corporate affairs departments. In the Nigerian context, this was a position of great influence, where you could easily award contracts arbitrarily and empower cronies. This was never the case at Guaranty Trust Bank. Throughout my time in this position, the leadership never tried to influence my team to take decisions contrary to, or in conflict with, the bank's values and policies. The recruitment process was never interfered with, and only the most qualified people were recruited. This paid off handsomely, as many of those young recruits are now in various leadership positions in both the private and public sectors. Today, these values—simplicity, professionalism, service, friendliness, excellence, trustworthiness, social responsibility, and innovation—have come to be known as the "Orange Rules." They continue to play a major role in the bank's success many years after Fola Adeola's exit.

My eight years at the bank played a significant role in shaping my values and has contributed in no small measure to the modest achievements I have recorded as an entrepreneur and as a leader. Anyone who is willing to adopt and consistently live by the values embodied in GT Bank's Orange Rules—either in their personal life or business affairs—is clearly on the path to genuine wealth creation. Adopting these values and making them an integral part of one's personal and professional life is imperative. Conversely, it is important to document the occasions when one falls short of these values. Challenges will arise in your quest to be true to these principles, especially from peers and the society at large, but it is important to remain strong and committed to your vows.

Character and integrity are well captured in the anthem of the Chartered Institute of Bankers of Nigeria (CIBN), which is "Chartered Institute of Bankers of Nigeria, the bankers guiding light. It's the nation's joy and pride. We aim for integrity in the industry. Uploading ethics and professionalism. Great! Great! CIBN. Citadel of excellence built on trust and honesty." Bankers know that the bedrock of the industry is integrity and character. If depositors and customers doubt the integrity of the bank, they won't do business with the bank. Likewise, if a bank doubts the character and integrity of any customer, they won't touch the customer. A part of the banker's creed reads as follows: "If you have reasons to distrust the integrity of a customer, close his account. Never deal with a rascal under the impression that you can prevent him from cheating you. The risk in such cases is greater than the profits." This creed is universally true not only for bankers but for everyone, whether dealing with a company or with individuals.

The story of the "Jewels under the Saddle" aptly captures the true meaning of integrity. A merchant, on a casual jaunt through a market, came across a fine specimen of a camel for sale. The merchant and the camel seller, both skilled negotiators, struck a hard bargain. The camel seller, pleased with his skill of worming out what he felt was a very good price, parted with his camel. The merchant, chuffed that he had struck a fantastic bargain, proudly walked home with the latest addition to his large livestock.

On arriving home, the merchant called to his servant to help him take out the camel's saddle. The servant found a small velvet pouch hidden under the saddle, which was filled with precious jewels. The servant was excited! "Master you bought a camel ... but see what came *free* along with it!"

The merchant was astonished as he looked at the jewels in his servant's palm. They were of extraordinary quality, sparkling and twinkling in the sunlight. "I bought the camel," he said, "not the jewels. I must return them to the camel seller immediately."

The servant was aghast. His master was being foolish. "Master ... no one will know," he said.

The merchant headed back to the market and handed the velvet pouch back to the camel seller. The camel seller was very happy. "I had forgotten that I hid these jewels in the saddle for safekeeping. Here, choose one of the jewels for yourself, as a reward."

The merchant said, "I paid a fair price for the camel and the camel only, so, no thank you, I do not need any reward."

As much as the merchant refused, the camel seller insisted. Finally, the merchant said, sheepishly smiling, "Actually, when I decided to bring the pouch back to you, I already took two of the most precious jewels and kept them for myself."

At this confession, the camel seller was a bit flabbergasted and quickly emptied the pouch to count the jewels. "All my jewels are here. What jewels did you keep?"

"The two most precious," said the merchant. "My integrity and my self-respect."

Personal and Financial Discipline

Self-discipline is a major distinction between people who succeed in life and those who do not. This is a concept that is generally taken for granted but is in fact fundamental to wealth creation. Successful people live a principle-centered life; they know that there are certain things you have to give up if you want to achieve greatness. Ultimately, what separates winners from losers is the ability for winners to conquer self. Napoleon Hill remarked, "If you do not conquer self, you will be conquered by self." Discipline matters in everything you do in life. You need self-discipline to stay healthy, to build a happy marriage, and to grow your finances.

In this social media age, young people are constantly bombarded with images and depictions of life that celebrate recklessness and flamboyance—a life without discipline or boundaries. Extravagance is portrayed as fashionable. This depiction could not be any further from the truth. It misrepresents the reality of life and has led millions of people astray. The moment a person allows himself to be distracted, the more likely the person ends up being poor.

The most vulnerable are talented people in sports and entertainment. The lives and careers of many great artists and sports personalities have been ruined because of a lack of self-discipline. Bad habits, if not overcome, will eventually bring you down, no matter what heights you attain. As the saying goes, you cannot be a winner with a loser's habit. Entrepreneur and author Jim Rohn remarked that "Success is nothing more than a few simple disciplines practiced every day." He also noted, "Discipline is the bridge between goals and accomplishments."

Discipline, not desire, determines your destiny. An important aspect of self-discipline is personal financial discipline. This is defined as a person's ability to achieve his or her goals through proper financial management. Most wealthy people have a disciplined financial lifestyle.

One of the simplest ways to understand wealth and poverty is to view it from the angle of income and expenditure. You can only become wealthy if your earning exceeds your expenses. Financial expert Dave Ramsey noted, "Financial peace is not the acquisition of stuff. It is learning to live on less than you make, so you can give money back and have money to invest. You cannot win until you do this."

One reason why expenses exceed income is the lack of a personal financial plan. Most people do not plan their finances, particularly if they are on a salaried income and live from paycheck to paycheck. It is common to see hardworking people struggle financially, running but not going anywhere. Although they work hard and earn a living, their lifestyle, lack of planning, and uncontrolled spending habits result in a perpetual cash flow crisis.

I received one of my most profound lessons on financial discipline from Fola Adeola, a cofounder of Guaranty Trust Bank. In 1994, I was promoted to the position of assistant general manager at the bank. I felt I needed to take advantage of my new entitlements and decided to move out of my two-bedroom flat to a more luxurious four-bedroom house in Ikoyi. After settling on what I considered a suitable house, I brought the request to him for his approval. After patiently listening to me, he counselled me against spending a huge amount on rent, when I had not built my own house, and advised me to wait until I was able to build my own home. He approved the loan, but after consulting with my wife, Jumoke, I decided to use the loan to buy a parcel of land instead. I ended up building my first house on the parcel of land. I sold the property for a very handsome profit many years later.

Benjamin Franklin said, "Beware of little expenses; a small leak will sink a great ship." Wealthy people meticulously plan their personal finances, control their spending, and are diligent about saving and investing. They remain in full control of their financial future and leave nothing to chance. Charles A. Jaffe wisely observed, "It is not your salary that makes you rich, it is your spending habits."

Keeping the Right Company

Keeping the right company is a critical factor in wealth creation. Moving with people who have the right mind-set about wealth can go a long way in furthering your own journey. The opposite is also true! Wealthy people are careful about who they associate with. Warren Buffett said, "Tell me who your heroes are, and I'll tell you how you'll turn out to be." Thomas C. Corley, author of *Change Your Habits, Change Your Life*, noted that in his five-year study of more than 150 millionaires, he found out that that "one of the hallmarks of wealthy, successful people was their ability to somehow break free of the human tendency to unconsciously forge relationships with others … Long before they became rich, the self-made rich made an intentional, conscious effort to only forge relationships with individuals they aspired to be: other rich and successful people."

Wealthy people see others in the same bracket as role models they can learn from. Associating with other wealthy people is also an opportunity to connect, benchmark, and bond with others in the same business or industry. Wealthy people share stories of success and information about new products or investment opportunities, stock tips, and other vital information that can make a major difference to one's fortunes. Information in financial circles is priceless, and being among wealthy people positions you to get information that can be financially rewarding.

On the contrary, people who are trapped in poverty like to associate with those whose thinking matches theirs. When a person is surrounded by negative forces, all you hear is resentment and anger. T Harv Eker said, "Resenting the rich is one of the surest ways to stay broke." So true! If you desire to be wealthy, then watch the company you keep.

While I was executive assistant to Otunba Subomi Balogun, I had the opportunity to meet and observe some notable corporate gurus, including Chief Chris Ogunbanjo, Chief Kola Daisi, Otunba Kunle Ojora, Chief Bade Ojora, and Alex Ibru (of blessed memory). These were some of the wealthiest people in Nigeria at the time, and the lessons I learned from observing and listening to them were vital in transforming my mind-set.

It was through keeping the right company that I became a part of one of the greatest corporate success stories in Nigeria's history.

One of my friends, Akin Akintoye, was a young lawyer and a friend to the founding members of Guaranty Trust Bank, and during one of my visits to his office, he discussed their formation plans with me. He subsequently introduced me to the principal promoters, Fola Adeola and Tayo Aderinokun. This connection led to one of the most important financial leaps in my entire life. Without Akin's referral, I would not have been introduced to Messrs Adeola and Aderinokun and would not have had the privilege of being a part of the bank's formation. Keeping the right company can be the difference between success and failure!

It is difficult to create wealth if you are surrounded by negative people. Negative people fill the atmosphere with doubt, suspicion, and fear. They grumble, gossip, backbite, and play the blame game. Stay away from such people. Associate with people who constantly motivate you to aim for higher things. Make friends with people who are doing great things! Eleanor Roosevelt once said, "Great minds discuss ideas; average minds discuss events; small minds discuss people." It was Charlie Jones who said, "You will be the same person in five years as you are today, except for the people you meet and the books you read."

Review your present relationships to determine which ones you should continue with and those you need to drop. Seek out the company of older and more successful people around you and ask them to mentor you. You can join social clubs, chambers of commerce, and trade associations, and you can also visit places and conferences where you are likely to meet highfliers, whose wealth of information and experience can make a difference in your life. I am not suggesting that you should shun your old friends who are struggling; I am simply encouraging you to cultivate relationships with people whose experience, counsel, and connections can motivate you to become better and more successful.

Find Your Passion

Passion is a prerequisite for wealth creation. Wealthy people are usually passionate people! According to Warren Buffett, "I will give you two pieces of advice. Invest as much in yourself as you can; you are your own best asset by far. Then follow your passion; you want to be really excited to get out of bed every morning." Buffet also noted, "Without passion, you do not have energy. Without energy, you have nothing." Ingrid Bergman, a Swedish actress and three-time Academy Award winner, said, "I've never sought success in order to get fame and money; it is the talent and the passion that counts in success."

If you derive pleasure from cooking, creating recipes, experimenting with spices, and catering to people's culinary needs, then one can conclude that you have a passion for cooking. You are more likely to succeed if you make a business out of this—by opening a restaurant, running an event catering company, or starting some other food business—than by doing any other business. Many people hate their jobs and businesses, and it is no wonder that they cannot make a success of it. They might have ventured into the job or business out of desperation. As a result, they are unlikely to have any passion for what they do. When passion is lacking, the results will be mediocre or, even worse, disastrous. "If you do not love what you do, you wouldn't do it with much conviction or passion," says Mariel Hamm, former American professional soccer player and two-time Olympic gold medalist.

A former classmate studied agricultural science at university but hated the course and barely graduated. After school, he took a job with a bank because the money was good. He did not enjoy banking and could not quite make a success of it. All along, he moonlighted as a disc jockey and organized parties and events during weekends. He really enjoyed this aspect of his life; it was his passion! He persisted with banking and retired after thirty years on the job into a life of penury. He was trapped in a job he had no passion for and ended up a poor person. During a discussion with him after he had retired, he expressed regret for not having pursued his passion for entertainment and building it into a thriving business.

There are several reasons why people stay in jobs they hate or continue to run businesses they are not passionate about. It can be a result of a seeming lack of options. There are those who are in business simply because they want to be their own boss. Others run businesses simply because they inherited it, and they feel they have no choice but to keep it going. In all these cases, there is a lack of passion to become an outstanding success. You are likely to succeed as an entrepreneur if you love what you do and if the thought of your business gets your juices flowing. Passion keeps you focused and excited about the possibility of creating something amazing. Pierre Omidyar, founder of eBay, once observed, "If you are passionate about something and you work hard, then I think you will be successful." Oprah Winfrey noted, "You have got to follow your passion. You have got to figure out what it is you love—who you really are. And have the courage to do that. I believe that the only courage anybody ever needs is the courage to follow your own dreams."

A friend of mine studied law and got a job in a law firm afterward. She disliked her job and was always unhappy and unfulfilled. She loved to create and design clothes for herself and her friends as a hobby. One day, she stumbled across a twelve-week training on fashion design. She took time off work and enrolled for the course. Today, her fashion house is rated as one of the top ten in Africa. Motivational speaker and writer Denis Waitley wrote, "Chase your passion, not your pension." Financial expert Dave Ramsey once said, "Passion is so key in leading and creating excellence that I will hire passion over education and talent every time." American preacher and entrepreneur T. D. Jakes noted, "If you cannot figure out your purpose, figure out your passion. For your passion will lead you right into your purpose." Celebrated poet and civil rights activist Maya Angelou once wrote, "You can only become truly accomplished at something you love. Do not make money your goal. Instead, pursue the things you love doing, and then do them so well that people can't take their eyes off you." In simple terms, make your passion your paycheck.

In his book *Homeless to Billionaire*, Andres Piras outlines some steps that can help in discovering your passion. According to him, if you are struggling to discover your passion, then you should start by answering these questions honestly: *On what subject can you read five hundred books without getting bored? What can you do for five straight years without getting paid for? What will you spend your time doing if you have the financial freedom to do anything you wish?* Dedication, commitment, and single-mindedness become much easier when you do what you love. Purpose is the reason we journey, and passion is the fire that lights the way.

A successful combination of passion and entrepreneurship can result in great achievement. Walter Chrysler, American industrialist, once said, "The real secret of success is enthusiasm. Yes, more than enthusiasm, I would say excitement. I like to see men get excited. When they get more excited, they make a success of their lives."

Steve Jobs, one of the great innovators and entrepreneurs of his generation, was raised by a father whose main job was tinkering with electronics in cars. As a result, Jobs developed an interest in electronics from an early age, and this continued to grow through high school all the way to college. He dreamed about transforming the world of consumer electronics, and he eventually succeeded through the creation of several breakthrough devices, including the iPod and subsequently the iPhone.

Find a Mentor

A mentor is someone who sees more talent and ability within you (than you see in yourself) and who helps bring it out of you. Mentorship is crucial to wealth creation. Indra Nooyi, former CEO of PepsiCo, remarked, "If I did not have mentors, I would not be here today. I am a product of great mentoring and great coaching. Coaches and mentors are very important." Oprah Winfrey observed, "For every one of us that succeeds, it is because there is somebody there to show you the way out." One of the greatest values of mentorship is the ability to see ahead through the lens of someone who has been where you want to go. Isaac Newton said, "If I have seen further, it is by standing on the shoulders of giants." A mentor is experienced in your line of business. He or she has been there before you, knows the peculiar challenges, and is willing to help you navigate its difficulties. A mentor will teach you how to think strategically, how to think long-term, how to handle challenges, how to cope with the cyclical nature of the market, and how to build customers and sales consistently.

I have been privileged to have great mentors throughout my career. In 1988, shortly after I joined First City Merchant Bank, Otunba Subomi Balogun spotted me and made me his executive assistant. Working closely with the first Nigerian to be granted a banking license and an entrepreneur who had substantial investments in oil and gas, manufacturing, real estate, and banking was beyond my wildest dreams. I recognized the opportunity for what it was and completely applied all my faculties to learn as much as I could from him. I was responsible for organizing his daily schedule, briefing him for his meetings, reviewing all files sent to him for approval, and taking notes during meetings. This is where I got my first schooling about the workings of executive meetings, strategies for winning in boardroom politics, elements of corporate governance, and many technical aspects of banking. All these lessons came in handy when I became a managing director and CEO of a bank. I learned a lot about wealth creation as I observed Otunba Balogun's investment strategies and dealmaking at close quarters. I emulated his immaculate sense of style, communication skills, negotiation skills, work ethic, leadership, and corporate governance skills.

When I was offered the opportunity to work at Guaranty Trust Bank as a senior manager in 1990, I promptly accepted. Breaking the news of my intended departure to my boss and mentor at FCMB was difficult. I pondered on it for days, until I finally summoned the courage once I sensed the atmosphere was conducive. He had just received our monthly financial performance report, which was very favorable, and I could see he was in a fine mood. He did not take the news very well, primarily because we recently lost top-notch staff to the newer banks. He eventually gave me his blessing, and I left FCMB with mixed feelings—sad that I had to leave a boss who I admired and saw as a mentor and father figure but joyful that I was blazing a trail with a set of determined young professionals.

Successful entrepreneurs are always willing to mentor young people if they see that they are focused, serious, diligent, discrete, purposeful, and persevering. Finding the right mentor is extremely important, even under circumstances where you are unable to work directly under them. Identify the right person in your desired field, approach them respectfully, and request to be a protégé.

Develop a Culture of Saving

George S. Clason, author of the classic best seller *The Richest Man in Babylon*, stated in respect to saving, "Wealth, like a tree, grows from a tiny seed. The first copper you save is the seed from which your tree of wealth shall grow. The sooner you plant that seed, the sooner shall the tree grow. The more faithfully you nourish and water that tree with consistent savings, the sooner may you bask in contentment beneath its shade. I found the road to wealth when I decided that a part of all I earned was mine to keep. And so, will you."

Saving is the practice of setting aside part of your earnings for future use. Viewed from another perspective, it is simply income not spent, or deferred consumption. Your dreams of becoming wealthy will be a mirage if you do not practice the discipline of saving. Methods of saving include putting money aside in a deposit account, a pension account, an investment fund, or as cash. It comes in several forms, but the most common is opening a savings account in a retail bank and depositing funds there to accumulate over time. Any form of interest-bearing account is technically a savings account: It might be an ordinary savings deposit, interest-bearing current account, fixed deposit, call account, or term deposit. These are variants of the same product. The most important element is that you set aside a part of your income to build wealth.

One significant way your savings can help in wealth creation is by being a source of start-up capital for your business. In fact, the most reliable source of personal equity for your new business is accumulated savings. Most people's business plans end at the stage where they need to raise capital. As you seek funding from other investors, family, and friends, one common question you will encounter is: how much money are you personally contributing to starting the business? This is a relevant question because it gives potential investors the confidence that you are a disciplined person and that you have skin in the game. In addition, your savings can be a source of funds for making investments in stocks, bonds, and other wealth instruments. Investing cannot happen without savings, unless you are among the fortunate few to have received a substantial bequest or won the lottery. Saving requires great discipline, but there are practical and attitudinal challenges that stand in the way of developing a saving culture. First, it takes a lot of willpower to forgo consumption and set money aside for future use. It is even more difficult when your earnings are lower than your expenses or when you are faced with tough decisions on spending that have an impact on other people, particularly your family and other dependents. The decision to save becomes even more complex when you factor in Nigeria's inflation rate, which is higher than the savings rate. Nigeria's annual inflation rate measured by the consumer price index was 11 percent in August 2019. This means that if you deposited ₦1,000 in the bank last year, it's actual worth is 11 percent less than what it was a year ago. In essence, your money depreciated within that period. This should normally be compensated for by the rate of interest you earn on your savings account, assuming the rate is equal to or higher than the rate of inflation. This is hardly the case in Nigeria and other developing countries. According to recent Central Bank statistics, the savings interest rate hovers at around 5 percent, which is significantly lower than the inflation rate. This factor is a major disincentive to those who want to save. In many developed economies, the reverse is usually the case: the inflation rate in the United States, for instance, has consistently been lower than the savings rate for years. In spite of this reality in Nigeria and other developing economies, it is still economically sensible to save, rather than to spend on nonessential items. The alternative to saving is consumption, because we spend the money we do not save.

The more fundamental problem has to do with mind-set. It just does not make sense to some people to save when they earn so little and have so many needs. If you take a survey of a hundred people from various socioeconomic backgrounds, fewer than 20 percent maintain savings in any form. Others acknowledge the importance of saving but admit that they simply cannot afford to. The erroneous belief is that only wealthy people—or people earning a high income—can afford to save. It is pertinent to stress that frugality is the path to wealth creation. Warren Buffet remarked, "Don't save what is left after spending; spend what is left after saving." An undisciplined financial lifestyle traps people in persistent financial troubles. Studies have shown that people are not always rational in the area of personal finance. They have limits to their self-control and are influenced by their own biases.

I recall being approached by someone for financial support to start a business venture. He was an employee of a manufacturing outfit but lost his job during the company's downsizing. When I inquired about his plans, I found out he had none: he wanted to start a business simply because he felt he had no other option. Worse still, he had no savings or investment. I advised him about how to start and run a business successfully. He was not interested in my counsel and simply wanted the loan. I told him that I would be willing to assist in starting the business on the condition that he showed me his savings of at least 10 percent of my intended contribution. He accused me of being uncaring. According to him, I was merely looking for an excuse to turn down his request. "How do you expect me to have savings when I earn so little?" he protested. I was patient with him because I could see that he was sincere in his ignorance. I explained to him that wealth creation, like planting a seed, requires discipline and patience. If you do not have the discipline to save, you will never be able to build wealth. I advised him to make sacrifices, including selling some of his assets, if he was committed to the new venture. I told him that I would only give my financial support after he invested his own money. Suffice to say, the gentleman did not come back, and the business venture never saw the light of day.

Anyone who can regularly save about 10 percent of their earnings must be commended, because impulsive spending is easier. It takes a disciplined and determined mind to deprive oneself of unnecessary consumption. Saving is a crucial step to getting out of the poverty cycle. No matter how little you earn, a part of it should be set aside for savings. The money you do not save will be spent on nonessentials—things you will likely be unable to account for.

Turn Your Idea into a Viable Business

Having discovered your passion, the next stage is to develop a business idea around it. If you want to succeed, you must make your own opportunities as you go. You may love music, but how can you build a profitable business around it? How do you convert your brilliance in architecture and passion for design into a successful architectural firm?

The ability to turn your passion into a business idea and then build a successful business out of it is what separates the wealthy from those who merely wish to be rich. Not everyone gets it right; in fact, the majority do not. The world is full of would-be and failed entrepreneurs who were unable to pivot their passion into successful businesses. This is primarily due to the inability to create or develop compelling products or services that people need or are willing to pay for.

The fact that you are passionate about something does not mean people will pay for it, irrespective of the way it is presented. You have to develop a game-changing product that can generate consumer demand. No matter how good your product or service is, if there is no demand, there will be no sales and, consequently, no viable business.

The story of MeCure Healthcare, a medical business enterprise started by medical professionals—Samir Udani, an Indian, and Kunle Adebowale, a Nigerian—in 2009, illustrates how successfully pivoting your passion or profession into a business can result in substantial wealth. MeCure offers a wide range of medical services—diagnostics, eye care, cardiac care, dental care, and fully integrated oncology services—and has now become a notable medical brand in Nigeria. MeCure has succeeded where many Nigerian doctors and medical centers have failed, because it has been able to successfully combine professional practice with entrepreneurship.

Find Your Path

The final principle involves defining your path to wealth creation. There are several proven paths to creating lasting wealth, and I have tried to present them as simply as possible. It is important to choose your path early in life. If you are in your twenties, for instance, a combination of entrepreneurship and investing is a great path to explore. At this age, you have enough time and energy to start a business and grow it to become a successful enterprise. If you are diligent and passionate and adhere to the foundational principles, you can own a business empire by the time you are forty. If you invest early, your portfolio will have grown significantly by this age.

1. **Build a Business Enterprise**

    This is the most prevalent path to wealth creation. To succeed in this, you must develop the proficiency and courage it takes to run a profitable business. Merely starting a business does not guarantee success and wealth. A large percentage of people trapped in poverty actually own businesses. Business owners who do not follow best practices and who lack the required passion and commitment to succeed will struggle financially.

2. **Invest in Assets, Equities, and Real Estate**

    Investing is one of the most strategic paths to building long-term wealth and financial security. It is the act of allocating funds to an asset or committing capital to an endeavor (a business, project, or real estate), with the expectation of generating income or profit. This is arguably the easiest path to attaining great wealth. Through investing, you acquire wealth assets that generate income and wealth without the exertion of extra effort on your part. As is often said, at this level of wealth creation, you do not work for money; your money works for you.

3. **A Combination of Entrepreneurship and Investing**

   This is the ultimate formula for wealth creation. About 90 percent of individuals on the Forbes list of the five hundred richest people in the world became wealthy through a combination of entrepreneurship and investing. Operated synergistically, you get the best out of both.

4. **Pursue a Career While You Invest in Assets, Equities, and Other Wealth Instruments**

   This path works most effectively for high-income earners such as executives of large corporations or well-paid professionals. To achieve this, you must start investing early in your career and master the art over time. As you climb the corporate ladder and your income increases significantly, you must be disciplined in managing your finances and resist the urge to spend wastefully. By the time you are at the peak of your career, your investments in quoted equities, real estate, and private equities will have grown to a level big enough to make you wealthy.

   Unfortunately, many top-flight executives and accomplished professionals struggle financially because they are ignorant or undisciplined.

Become an Apprentice

There are several successful entrepreneurs who went straight into business without ever working for anyone and made a huge success of it. In truth, this is the exception to the rule. Working as an employee prior to venturing into business is typically an important step. Entrepreneurship involves a lot of risk-taking and requires a certain level of knowledge and experience. As soon as you have a clear vision of your path and your passion, working for an organization where you can get the valuable experience, exposure, knowledge, and connections that will prepare you for your own entrepreneurial ambitions is a must.

Sometime in 2010, I had a lengthy discussion with the late Tayo Aderinokun, a cofounder of Guaranty Trust Bank. He was a wealthy banker and successful entrepreneur and investor who owned considerable interests in real estate, financial services, banking, and education. He was also a generous patron to numerous causes. I was fascinated by his extensive business interests and wanted to know how he had been able to build so much wealth at a young age. He explained that he chose his path early. He developed a passion for entrepreneurship at the age of twenty-three, while he was an MBA student at the University of California. Upon his return to Nigeria, he worked at Chase Merchant Bank, where he honed his skills in credit, core banking, and investing. He rose to become the head of credit and marketing and was also a branch manager for a while. He subsequently moved to Prime Merchant bank, one of the "new generation" banks, as assistant general manager. He resigned less than a year into the job and started his own financial services company, First Marina Trust Company.

At this point, he became a full-fledged entrepreneur. He teamed up with his friend and colleague, Fola Adeola, to actualize his dream of establishing a bank. Tayo told me that his time at Chase prepared him for his leadership role at Guaranty Trust. It allowed him to explore the dynamics of the world of banking, investing, and real estate. He noted that working his way up the corporate ladder and subsequently managing his own financial-service company prepared him for his role in cofounding and leading Guaranty Trust.

The apprenticeship or protégé phase is a crucial learning stage in the blueprint for wealth creation. This is where you gain the hands-on experience in the art of running a successful business. This is the stage where you acquire knowledge, save up capital, and plan toward the next stage of wealth creation. A lot of people idle away because they are unable to secure their dream job. Most young people are searching for jobs in oil companies, telecommunication, and government parastatals in the oil and gas sector, banks and financial institutions, customs and immigration sectors, and other areas they consider juicy. The only thing these jobs have in common is money. It is either the pay is great, or there is the belief that there are opportunities to make money on the side. The drive for many young people is *money*. This kind of thinking comes from erroneous ideas about money. Having money does not amount to being wealthy, and the passion for money leads nowhere. A person's primary goal should not be to simply accumulate money.

It should be apprenticeship. Securing a high-profile establishment job should not be your goal unless it matches your passion and plans. You should choose a job that fits into your dreams and ideas, so that you can learn the fundamentals of your chosen career. It requires a lot of sacrifice and patience.

The second habit in Stephen Covey's classic, *The 7 Habits of Highly Effective People*, is "begin with the end in mind." He explains that "to begin with the end in mind means to start with a clear understanding of your destination." It means to have an appreciation of where you are now, knowing where you are going, and ensuring that every step taken is toward that destination. The benefits of being an employee for a period cannot be overemphasized. During this period, the urge to start your own business will arise, often prematurely. This is a common trap many people fall into, due to a lack of adequate preparation.

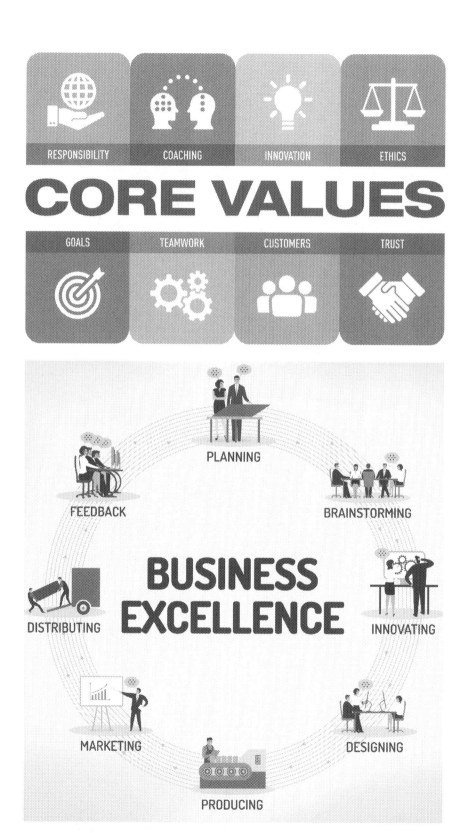

CHAPTER 6

The Fundamentals of Entrepreneurship

He who is not courageous enough to take risks will accomplish nothing in life.

—Mohammed Ali

All our dreams can come true, if we have the courage to pursue them.

—Walt Disney

Your mind is made up about creating wealth. You are committed to adopting a positive wealth mind-set. You are willing to embrace financial discipline. You have reevaluated your relationships, and you have made the decision to be a person of integrity. At this stage, you have identified a mentor and you are on a pathway to creating wealth for yourself. If you decide to embark on the journey of running a successful business that will propel you to the realms of financial security, this chapter is meant to guide you and propel you toward your goal of becoming a wealthy entrepreneur.

Entrepreneurship is synonymous with business ownership. It is the art of developing, organizing, and managing a business enterprise for profit. It is a time-tested way of creating wealth and the surest way to financial success.

Nigeria is blessed with a rich history of daring but successful entrepreneurial stories. For every entrepreneur, getting started can be overwhelming. It is important for entrepreneurs to start small, with the big picture in mind. One of the great entrepreneurs of the colonial era was Adeola Odutola, who was a trader in cocoa, yam, cassava, cattle, timber, and tire treads. In 1967, he set up a factory to manufacture bicycles, motorcycles, tires, and tubes, becoming the first Nigerian company to manufacture these products. He faced a lot of opposition from the colonial government but remained undaunted and built one of the most successful business enterprises of that era.

Other notable entrepreneurs of that generation include Odumegwu Ojukwu, Aminu Dantata, and Henry Fajemirokun. These were Nigerians who blazed the trail at a time when foreign companies dominated commerce and industry, and at a time when British economic interest was the focus of the colonial administration. Some of those who have made giant entrepreneurial strides in more recent times include Aliko Dangote (commodities); Mike Adenuga (telecom, oil, real estate); Otunba Subomi Balogun and Jim Ovia (banking and real estate); Tony Elumelu, Aig Imoukhuede, and Herbert Wigwe (banking); Femi Otedola (oil); Razak Okoya (manufacturing, real estate); Abdulsamad Rabiu (commodities); Folorunsho Alakija (oil); Jason Njoku (media); Stella Okoli (pharmaceutical); Nnamdi Ezeigbo (telecoms); Leo Stan Ekeh (e-commerce and information technology), among others. These successful Nigerian entrepreneurs are not spirits. They are like you and I. If they could achieve so much success, you and I can do the same. We just need to do the right thing and follow the rules as detailed earlier. I have interacted with many of these successful entrepreneurs and have found out that what separates some of them from the rest of us are as simple as those rules of wealth I highlighted in the last chapter

I recently commissioned a survey on entrepreneurship in Nigeria. The results were revealing and will serve as a guide to those who are currently entrepreneurs, or those who are planning to venture into entrepreneurship. Lack of data has been identified as a major cause of business failure in Nigeria, and I am hoping this can serve as a conversation starter.

The sample size was five hundred entrepreneurs across the entire country, cutting across different age groups and sectors of the economy. Based on the parameters as defined in this book, a staggering 85 percent of respondents are either trapped in poverty or struggling financially. The survey revealed that these entrepreneurs attributed their ongoing struggles to several factors, including inadequate and expensive sources of funding (high interest rates and the reluctance of banks to support their businesses); stifling government regulations, multiple taxation and bureaucratic red tape; poor power and transportation infrastructure and, for local manufacturers, an unfavorable import regime (including smuggling and dumping of inferior products).

Diving deeper into their troubles actually revealed a startling finding. The core factors truly responsible for their struggles include the following: the lack of basic business skills (including entrepreneurial training); low level of technology adoption; substandard products and services, including branding and packaging; limited access to market; weak corporate governance; poor record keeping and general financial mismanagement.

A critical look at the 15 percent of respondents who can be classified as wealthy and successful highlights a fundamental difference. This point is particularly poignant because the survey revealed that the keys to their successes include the following: a well-articulated and implemented business plan, a well-structured business enterprise, and a motivated workforce. In addition, personal attributes like courage, creativity, determination, passion, integrity, reliability, patience, accountability, and responsibility feature prominently in their success stories.

Curiously, successful entrepreneurs have developed ways of navigating around the same tough business environment highlighted by the struggling entrepreneurs. They affirmed their journeys have brought them immense pride and a sense of fulfilment and also expressed confidence in the future.

It is important for aspiring young entrepreneurs to note that success knows no age or sector barrier. Out of the wealthy 15 percent, approximately 58 percent of the entrepreneurs fall within the ages of thirty-five and fifty-five, and 12 percent are between twenty and twenty-five years of age. Forty percent are into trading and merchandising; 25 percent are into real estate; 15 percent operate in financial services; and 5 percent are into manufacturing and agriculture. A majority—65 percent—own or have invested in multiple businesses.

The majority of the wealthy entrepreneurs between twenty and twenty-five years of age are into information technology and related businesses and different aspects of the telecommunication business. More importantly, a significant majority of the younger entrepreneurs were mentored by, or worked with, older and more accomplished professionals before starting their own companies.

All hope is not lost for the 85 percent category of struggling entrepreneurs. Adopting the blueprint for wealth creation (as highlighted in the last chapter) is a critical first step. Irrespective of whether you are a new, existing, successful, or struggling business, the following steps will change the trajectory of your business exploits and will propel you to unimaginable heights.

Creativity and Innovation

> Imagination is envisioning things that do not exist. Creativity is applying imagination to address a challenge. Innovation is using creativity to generate unique solutions. Entrepreneurship is applying innovations and scaling the ideas by inspiring others.
>
> —Tina Seelig

In early 1989, when I got involved in the formation of Guaranty Trust Bank, I immediately realized that the principal promoters, Fola Adeola and Tayo Aderinokun, were clear about their intention of creating a first-class bank. They envisioned a service-oriented and technology-driven bank built on solid corporate governance, excellence, and innovation. The preoperation activities started about eighteen months before the bank commenced business. During this period and while the banking license was being processed, the promoters met regularly to brainstorm on various aspects of the proposed bank, including the operational blueprint, visioning, marketing and business strategies, and the core values and culture of the bank. Employees were recruited through a rigorous and merit-driven process. Most of the new hires were young and fresh graduates, while a few were middle-level managers handpicked from existing banks. The plan was to assemble a core team of competent and resourceful young men and women who could be trained to embrace the radical vison of the new bank.

Guaranty Trust Bank disrupted the Nigerian banking sector in 1991 with its unique and revolutionary banking halls, open teller system, and real-time banking. These were features that had never been tried in the Nigerian banking sector, and nobody was sure of how it would be received. Prior to this, banks operated a manual or semiautomated system of handling deposits and payments in the banking halls. Prior to cashing checks, customers collected a tag or number and waited for hours before being able to see a teller. Upon receipt of the check, the teller—usually caged behind a glass compartment—would take the check to a back office for authentication, signature verification, balance confirmation, identification verification, and approval of payment by several layers of officers. All this was done manually using registers, signature cards, and account ledgers. Aside from being cumbersome and time-consuming, this method was also susceptible to fraud and errors. Guaranty Trust Bank bundled these different processes into a single operation with a banking software called Standard Banking Software (SBS) technology. The software enabled the bank to capture the customer's signature, photograph, and account balance in one module and then update the account balance in real time after every transaction. The bank also removed the glass cubicles and introduced open teller counters, where the customer and the officer interacted without any barriers. It reduced the average banking time by more than twenty minutes. The banking halls were considered to be one of the most elegant in the industry and were equipped with state-of-the-art technology. These innovations took the industry by surprise, and customers were fascinated by the radical transformation in the banking experience. Many of the new generation banks quickly adopted similar systems and processes, while the older banks were caught napping and scrambled to compete. Guaranty Trust Bank disrupted the industry with its bold and creative endeavors and caused a stir that changed the banking industry forever.

One of the most important tasks of an entrepreneur is identifying business opportunities and developing successful products around it. A business opportunity exists when there is a need that consumers require for existence, survival, or convenience, and it can potentially be met by a new product or service. The entrepreneur's responsibility is to provide a solution to such needs or wants and to create an enterprise in the process. This is the foundation of most successful businesses.

Boeing and Airbus are the world's largest manufacturers of jetliners: they provide a solution to the problem of long-distance travel. Apple, Samsung, and Huawei are the world's largest producers of smartphones: they solve the problem of communication, entertainment, and financial transaction for billions of people. Netflix has disrupted the home video business, making a significant dent in DVD sales and putting conventional movie rental companies out of business. Amazon and companies like Flipkart in India and Konga in Nigeria have disrupted the global retail industry. Traditional retail giants like JCPenney, Sears, Woolworths, and Macy's are witnessing a rapid decline in sales and have had to close hundreds of outlets. A business will only survive and grow if its solutions continuously meet the needs of consumers.

Identifying opportunities and turning them into business solutions is at the core of entrepreneurship. Physicist William Pollard observed, "Without change, there is no innovation, creativity, or incentive for improvement. Those who initiate change will have a better opportunity to manage the change that is inevitable." IBM president Ginni Rometty remarked that "The only way you survive is to continuously transform into something else. It is this idea of continuous transformation that makes you an innovation company." Tesla founder Elon Musk noted, "Starting and growing a business is as much about the innovation, drive and determination of the people who do it as it is about the product they sell." Management guru Peter Drucker remarked, "Innovation is the specific instrument of entrepreneurship. It is the act that endows resources with a new capacity to create wealth."

At every level, a successful business must be able to capture consumers' attention with unique products and services that outperform the competition. The entrepreneur must spend a lot of time thinking, researching, and strategizing to create game-changing products and services. As a young entrepreneur, one should pursue ventures that will fundamentally change one's community, industry, country, or even the world. Inspiration should be drawn from individuals and companies that have fundamentally transformed how we live. Apple's iPhone disrupted the mobile phone industry. Netflix and YouTube disrupted the home video industry. Amazon, eBay, and Alibaba have transformed the world of retailing. Facebook, Instagram, Snapchat, and WhatsApp have reinvented the way we socialize and communicate. These companies created revolutionary products and have in turn generated billions of dollars in profit. One of the most fascinating stories in modern business history is that of Uber. Uber was born out of the determination of two young men—Travis Kalanick and Garret Camp—to solve the problem of a shortage of taxi cabs in urban and nonurban areas at odd hours. The idea that would later become Uber was first mooted after they struggled to find a cab one night after attending a technology conference. Camp returned to California with the idea floating in his head. He registered the domain name and teamed up with Kalanick. Uber has revolutionized the transport industry on a global scale and is now worth billions of dollars. The example of the founders of Uber affirms the power of creativity and innovation in wealth creation. As a young entrepreneur, you should think and dream big. Broaden your outlook through travel, read books and journals on creativity and invention, and attend conferences, particularly in one's area of business.

There are countless business opportunities that the internet and social media in particular have made possible. For instance, there is a huge opportunity in e-commerce. Konga, a Nigerian e-commerce giant that was founded in 2012, has expanded far beyond the dream of its founder, Sim Shagaya, and was recently sold for more than $10 million. Konga's success is not unique. A significant number of internet start-ups are springing up daily in Nigeria. One example is Jobberman—an online job portal created by Opeyemi Awoyemi, Ayodeji Adewunmi, and Olalekan Olude while they were undergraduates at the Obafemi Awolowo University, Ile-Ife. The idea was to develop a job portal to connect young graduates seeking jobs and employers looking for the best talents. Jobberman was an idea born of necessity. As Awoyemi recalled, "The idea came to me while in my third year in the university. I shared it with a few friends and course mates, and we discussed it passionately." Shortly after that, he bought the domain name jobberman.com and launched the website. The trio of Awoyemi, Adewunmi, and Olude formally launched the company in August 2009. "We did not put a particular amount of money together," says Awoyemi about the initial investment into the company. "We pretty much started with what we had, and gradually scaled. For the first eight months, all the money invested in the business was less than ₦300,000; it all came from our pocket money and savings."

After graduating, the trio moved to Lagos because it had the largest concentration of employers of any Nigerian state. It was also an opportunity to have direct access to mentors and potential investors. The company received a major boost the following year, when it attracted the attention of a venture capital firm—Tiger Global Management—through which it raised its first round of funding, $1 million. It is interesting to note that the investors reached out first and not the other way around. The injection of capital was a major milestone for the company; it provided a much-needed cash boost to finance its operations, invest in infrastructure, and recruit capable hands. "To say it was a smooth journey would be a lie," noted Awoyemi. "This is Nigeria, it is not easy. But frankly, these are exciting times to live and build a business here. This is a virgin market, and I would do it over and over again. Nigeria is what the economists call a frontier market and there is no better place to do business than in frontier markets. It took total commitment, focus, immense energy and the grace of God to grow the business in the face of daunting challenges. Sometimes it really seemed impossible, but we kept pushing."

At inception, the company was faced with many adverse circumstances, but the doggedness and determination of these young men enabled them to survive. For a long time, they were shunned by banks and could not access credit facilities; they had to survive by bootstrapping. When it became too costly to physically visit employers, they turned to digital tools—email, social media, and telesales. They also started with low-hanging fruits, like small businesses without a hiring budget, and over time, they acquired large businesses and corporations as clients.

BellaNaija is an online media enterprise that was started by Uche Pedro more than ten years ago. At that time, Uche was an employee of Cadbury Plc but was determined to start her blogging business at the time when the industry was at its infancy stages in Nigeria. A combination of determination, persistence, focus, industry, and perseverance was responsible for the transformation of BellaNaija from a relatively unknown blog to one of Nigeria's most successful online media companies in this generation.

Jobberman's and BellaNaija's stories, among many others, should be an inspiration to young men and women who are in business but are struggling to keep it going. Courage, innovation, and determination are required to create the next Konga, Jumia, BellaNaija. or Jobberman. Management guru Peter Drucker once said the following:

> Innovation is the specific tool of entrepreneurs, the means by which they exploit change as an opportunity for a different business or a different service. It is capable of being presented as a discipline, capable of being learned and capable of being practiced.
>
> Entrepreneurs need to search purposefully for the sources of innovation, the changes and their symptoms that indicate opportunities for successful innovation. And they need to know and to apply the principles of successful innovation.

As a guide, make sure your business idea is sustainable and scalable, because the business world is constantly evolving.

Many companies and products that dominated the landscape thirty years ago have been vanquished by new technologies. Kodak dominated the business of photography but ran into problems because they did not make the transition to digital photography quickly enough. Nokia and Erickson were the leaders in mobile telephony but were overtaken by Apple and Samsung. Uber did not exist ten years ago but now dominates the taxi businesses in many countries. AirBnB is a home rental start-up that has grown to become a major threat to the biggest hotel chains. The entrepreneurship landscape was once dominated by industrial and manufacturing giants like General Electric, General Motors, Ford, Toyota, Boeing, Sony, Exxon Mobil, and Shell. The most dominant companies today are Apple, Amazon, Facebook, Walmart, and Google. We cannot say for sure what the future holds, but one thing that is certain is that innovation and creativity will be at the epicenter of the evolution of the most dominant businesses globally—Nigeria included.

A Solid Business Plan

If you fail to plan, you are planning to fail!
—Benjamin Franklin

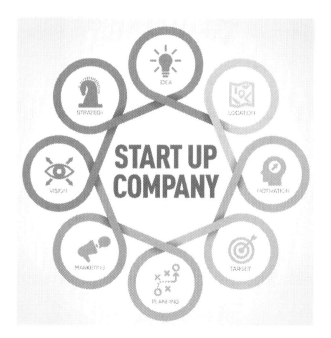

The next step for any aspiring entrepreneur is the creation of a business plan. A business plan is a written document that describes in detail how a business—usually a new one—intends to achieve its goals. A business plan lays out a written plan from a marketing, financial, and operational viewpoint.

The business plan is a road map that gives the business the direction and steps to take to achieve a predetermined goal. It articulates the vision, mission, and short- and long-term goals. It defines the strategies for production, marketing, hiring, and financing. The business plan is like a GPS that maps out the direction of the business over a period.

One of the most important functions of the business plan is that it is a tool for raising capital. Potential investors—venture capitalists, lenders, and friends and family—will require a business plan to evaluate the potentials of the business before making funding decisions. Depending on your level of expertise, you can prepare the plan in-house with your planning manager or financial controller, or you can engage the services of professionals who will work with you and your team.

Certain steps are taken before writing the business plan. This includes conducting research on the business and preparing a feasibility report on its prospects, its peculiar challenges, and its competitors. Upon completion of these preliminary activities, you will have gained a better knowledge of the business environment, competition, and other important information.

Preparing a business plan is in itself an intensive process that requires the use of analytical tools and trends and covers in detail critical areas like a marketing plan, operational plan, management and organization structure, financing structure, and capitalization plan. This is the phase where the business's unique products and services and target market must be clearly defined. The plan is crucial to the survival of the business, particularly at the early stages, because it prepares the entrepreneur to think and act strategically. It is also an implementation tool needed to navigate critical junctures during the takeoff period. For instance, the business might require certain licenses and regulatory approvals, which may cause undue delays and may prove costly if not timed properly. A business plan will outline all the steps required to avoid such complications. The plan serves as a yardstick to measure the company's actual performance. Besides the owner, other stakeholders, such as lenders and financiers, can use it to monitor the progress of the business.

In the early days of Guaranty Trust Bank, we converted our business plan into a monthly performance review (MPR) document. This broke down the bank's financial statement and compared the performance of each month with the stated budget projection. This was helpful in monitoring the performance of the various departments, products, and projects. It enabled the bank to consistently monitor and promptly identify its strengths, weaknesses, opportunities, threats from competitors, market fluctuation, employee performance, and resource constraints. It worked so effectively that other banks adopted it as part of their management tool. Many years later, when I was the deputy governor and chairman of the Revenue Mobilization Committee of the Lagos State Government, we used the MPR tool to great effect in driving the growth of the state's internally generated revenue. The results were astounding.

A Solid Financial Structure and Plan

In 1997, after seven years of growth in Guaranty Trust Bank, I felt financially comfortable, and I was prepared to pursue my dream of becoming a full-time entrepreneur. I had a vision of owning a financial-services company, and I was sure I had the requisite passion, experience, and knowledge to succeed at it. I resigned my appointment at Guaranty Trust Bank in December 1997. This was a high point in my banking career, and I felt prepared to begin a new life as an entrepreneur. I registered a company, Tower Capital Finance, sometime at the beginning of 1998 and was set to begin operation within six months. I needed that period to prepare adequately, draw up a business plan, rent an office space, and recruit capable hands. As fate would have it, at that very moment, I was invited for a private meeting with a director of a struggling bank to discuss the possibility of an acquisition.

In the same year, I teamed up with three colleagues—Olorogun O'tega Emerhor, Akin Adetola, and Patrick Bassey—to acquire the now defunct Comet Merchant Bank from its previous owners. This acquisition was as a result of the inability of the owners to raise the ₦500 million minimum share capital as stipulated by a new CBN policy on merchant banks. I was appointed the MD/CEO after the acquisition. I took over a bank that did not have the best of personnel. It was poorly capitalized and had a weak customer base with little or no brand recognition. If the bank was to be repositioned to compete effectively, it was clear to us that the workforce had to be reorganized. I immediately constituted a team comprised of myself, Patrick Bassey (a codirector), and the head of personnel of the bank. The goal was to assemble a top-class workforce with the requisite skill set, experience, entrepreneurial drive, right values, and a culture of excellence. Within days, we reached the painful conclusion that 95 percent of the workforce had to go. Simultaneously, we decided to embark on the recruitment of new employees to replace them. Breaking the news to these employees was difficult; it was probably the toughest exercise I ever embarked on in my professional career. These were young men and women who had devoted many years of their lives to the organization and who had no other means of livelihood.

Due to the sensitivity of the assignment, I handled the responsibility on a one-on-one basis with most of them. I spread out the assignment over a three-month period to minimize the disruption of the bank's everyday business, to ensure that it was carried out with the utmost discretion. Second, I approved a generous severance package for each employee to ease the pain. Third, I engaged a consultant to organize a workshop for the departing employees to help them with their transition process.

The next major challenge involved the recruitment of replacements. We prepared a business plan for the reorganization and repositioning of the bank, which had a section on the new organizational structure, staffing requirements, and compensation package. As the CEO and co-owner of the bank, I was clear about the people I wanted on my team. I identified the critical functions and prioritized my recruitment goals. To fill the most strategic positions, I had to poach from an institution I trusted—Guaranty Trust Bank. Convincing an employee of Guaranty Trust to leave a stable job for an unknown, weak and unstable bank was a daunting task, but what helped was that I was an alumnus of the bank. I adopted the Guaranty Trust template, which I had helped design when I was head of corporate services at the bank. It was a recruitment philosophy strictly based on merit: it started with an aptitude test, followed by interviews, and finalized with a weeklong training and workshop. I resisted every attempt from shareholders, board members, friends, family, and others to influence the recruitment process.

All the effort paid off, and we filled all the strategic and sensitive positions within four months of acquiring the bank. We recruited talented and resourceful graduates. Today, many of them are successful CEOs and senior managers in banking and other industries. Within a short period, the bank successfully transitioned from a little-known merchant bank to a brand-name technology-driven retail bank that we renamed as First Atlantic Bank. It was the first Nigerian bank to introduce internet banking, with a flagship product called *Flash me Cash*.

I poured my whole heart and creative energy into building the bank. I knew failure was not an option. I had no hesitation to commit much of my wealth into this new venture. It was a huge risk but a calculated one: I was the chief executive officer, and I knew I would give everything to make the venture a success. We had converted our status to that of a universal bank and embarked on a major reorganization and repositioning. Now, I was not just an owner/manager but an owner with substantial holdings and also the CEO. It was more rewarding than anything I had ever done, and I owe it all to strategic planning. First Atlantic was later acquired by FCMB, after growing its capital base and market share. This was only possible due to a well-thought-out plan from the onset.

A well-defined financial plan is crucial to the success of any business enterprise. As is often said, cash flow is the lifeblood of any business, and the lack of it, particularly at critical moments, can be disastrous. Entrepreneurs must exploit every possible source of funding to ensure that cash flow is always adequate. Your business plan should include a detailed financial plan, highlighting your projected revenue, balance sheet, cash flow, and capital structure. Your capital structure will focus on initial capital requirements and sources of funds for capital assets and operations. The capital structure will also indicate the proportion of your starting capital that will be personally contributed, the proportion that will be loaned, and the portion that will come from individual or institutional investors. The apportioning will be dependent on how much of the money you can personally provide and how much control you are willing to cede to investors. If you are unable to provide enough capital to give you controlling shares of the company, you may have no choice but to involve outsiders who may be individual investors, venture capitalists, or angel investors. However, relying too heavily on outside equity may be detrimental to the vision of the entrepreneur, as they stand the risk of losing control of the company to outsiders.

The case of Steve Jobs is worth mentioning here. When Steve Jobs and Stephen Wozniak started Apple, they were young and had no money. They could not raise debt capital and had to give up a chunk of the ownership of their company to outsiders to enable them to access much-needed capital. Apple experienced significant growth in the early 1980s, and in order to position it for greater success, it hired PepsiCo CEO, John Sculley, to lead the company. Jobs remained as COO so he could focus on product creation and design.

A few years later, a major dispute—essentially a power struggle over the direction and control of the company—arose between Jobs and Sculley. Jobs was a minority shareholder in the business he founded because he had sold a chunk of shares to outside investors. As a result, he was outvoted and fired from the company. Jobs left Apple to start a new company, NeXT. It did so well that Jobs convinced Apple to acquire it for a huge sum about a decade later. Fortunately for Jobs, more than a decade after his ouster, he was able to return to lead Apple and reinvented it to become one of the most valuable companies in the world.

In truth, not many cases have such a happy ending. There are so many instances of entrepreneurs losing their companies mainly because of a flaw in the capital structure. Professional support is important when structuring one's capital, as it ensures adequate protection in the event that the company becomes very successful.

Robust Marketing and Sales Strategy

Marketing refers to activities undertaken by a company to promote the buying and selling of a product or service. It is the means through which you communicate with your potential customers to convince them to connect with you and buy your product or service. Marketing includes advertising, selling, and delivering products to consumers or other businesses.

Every entrepreneur must pay special attention to this crucial and fundamental aspect of a business enterprise. Without a market, there can be no sales, and without sales, there can be no revenue. You cannot sell your product—no matter how good it is—if you do not get into the minds and pockets of your potential customers. Connecting with your customer means you know and understand the product or service that fits the customer's specific needs and wants.

A number of steps have to be taken for effective marketing to take place. Market research is a must, whenever a product or service is being conceptualized at the early stages. This helps one ascertain whether there is indeed a market. Depending on the business's size and financial capability, market research can be outsourced to a professional firm or handled by the staff of the company. Market research will help the entrepreneur determine who its potential customers are and how to connect with them. It also provides vital information about the competition, so that the company fully appreciates what it is up against. The information gathered from market research allows a company to develop an effective marketing plan.

The first step in creating an effective marketing plan is to determine your marketing goals. A simple marketing goal can be to gain a 10 percent share of the target market within a year. The next step will be to formulate an action plan required to achieve the goal. What is commonly known as the five Ps of marketing can be a very useful tool in crafting your strategy. These are as follows:

People: Your target customers. Who are these customers? Where are they located? What exactly do they want?

Product: How best do I connect my product with these people, and how does my product meet the needs of my target customers?

Place: Where will my potential customers find my product? In what ways and through which media can I get them to connect with the product? A physical store? Online? Direct marketing to their homes or offices?

Price: What price will the people consider reasonable? At what price can I stay competitive while remaining profitable?

Promotion: What are the most effective ways of promoting my products? How do I distinguish my product from the competition?

All these elements are crucial in marketing and ensuring effective connection with your customers. This aspect of the business is fundamental, so it is generally advisable to engage professionals to help with crafting strategy, while employing competent staff to implement them.

A Motivated and United Workforce

> Talent wins games, but teamwork and intelligence win championships.
>
> —Michael Jordan

The quality of your personnel is key to the success of your business. From the onset, entrepreneurs must engage the right set of people and be prepared to remunerate, motivate, and incentivize them at the prevailing market rate. Many entrepreneurs shortchange their businesses by hiring family members, friends, or poorly trained personnel to save cost. As the saying goes, if you pay peanuts, you get monkeys. Any entrepreneur that intends to succeed and create wealth needs to be skillful in forging a great team. You cannot produce great results without a great team. Andrew Carnegie observed, "Teamwork is the ability to work together toward a common vision, and the ability to direct individual accomplishments toward organizational objectives. It is the fuel that allows common people to attain uncommon results."

Hiring the right employees at the onset is important to the survival of your business, and if handled efficiently, it can be the difference between a one-man shop and a multibillion-naira corporation. A founder/CEO needs to start off with a team. Engaging a partner, consultant, and possibly a few employees to team up with you to execute your vision and plan is a must. You cannot be an expert in every area, so you need other people to help you with recruitment, financial planning and control, sales and marketing, engineering and production, operations, and many other aspects of the business.

The business plan should spell out the organizational structure and how decisions are made across the business. It defines how activities such as task allocation, coordination, and supervision are geared toward the achievement of the organization's goals. The structure should indicate the number of employees required, their job titles, responsibilities and duties, and possibly the recommended pay for each role. The conventional wisdom is to start light and avoid too many employees at the onset, because a bloated staff leads to higher personnel and administrative costs. A delicate balance must be maintained, because it is very easy to end up shortchanging the business by hiring fewer than necessary personnel, or by not paying enough to attract the best talent. The ideal balance is to hire talented people into key positions at the start, while motivating them with an attractive pay and other perks.

Making use of outside consultants to handle strategic functions such as legal, secretarial, accounting, auditing, and information technology operations is imperative. Hiring part-time/outsourced personnel to handle less strategic functions such as sales, marketing, and customer service is also important. A robust software can eliminate the need for many employees in accounts, marketing, sales, and other line positions. After the decision has been made about *who* to hire, the next step is determining *how* to hire. For a small start-up with very few employees, the owner has to be personally involved in the hiring process, particularly for strategic positions. This is to ensure that new hires are the best fit for the organization's values and strategy.

Alternatively, engaging experienced human resource professionals to oversee the internal process can be beneficial. A third option is to hire a human resource management company for the entire process. Finally, it is important to note that the total amount of compensation impacts the bottom line, because it is a contractual commitment. Once a letter of offer is issued and accepted, it becomes binding on the entrepreneur.

CHAPTER 7

Money Earns Money

Compound interest is the eighth wonder of the world.
He who understands it, earns it. He who doesn't, pays it.
—Albert Einstein

Real estate cannot be lost or stolen, nor can it be carried
away. Purchased with common sense, paid for in full,
and managed with reasonable care, it is about the safest
investment in the world.
—Franklin D. Roosevelt

Sometime in 1989, a friend of mine introduced me to a group of young
professionals who were desirous of establishing a bank. I worked alongside
the two principal promoters, Fola Adeola and Tayo Aderinokun,
supported by a host of equally committed young professionals, including
Akin Akintoye, Gbolahan Osibodu, Jimi Agbaje, Bode Agusto, Femi
Akingbe, and Babatunde Dabiri, among others.

I was impressed by their determination, confidence, courage, vision,
and sense of purpose. I wanted to be part of the journey, and I was
offered the shares directly (no private equity firm was involved). The
minimum share subscription offered was ₦200,000 ($45,000 at the

time) at ₦1 per share. This amount was more than five times my annual salary! I had no substantial savings and investment in equities or real estate to raise the cash, but I was determined to subscribe within the stipulated time frame. My mind was made up; I was not going to miss the unique opportunity. I approached my employer for a personal loan of ₦35,000—the maximum I was entitled to—and promptly paid into the account of First Marina Trust (the company handling the banking license and payment). Within a few weeks of receiving the offer letter, I had been able to pay about 25 percent of the total required. Afterward, I scraped together every kobo I could from my salary and allowances, but I was still a long way from meeting the target. A few weeks to the deadline, I was finally able to pay the balance after securing additional funding under agreed-upon conditions.

I have recounted this experience to illustrate the zeal, determination, and commitment required for wealth creation. I was determined to invest in the new enterprise, and I was willing to make sacrifices to realize my dream. This investment turned out to be a breakthrough for me in terms of wealth creation, and it was only possible because I seized the moment.

I resumed as the first fully employed staff of Guaranty Trust Bank in August 1990 and immediately became an owner-manager in a banking institution, a very rare opportunity in those days. From August 1990 (when the bank opened for business) up until 1996, it operated as a private bank, and dividends were paid twice a year. The bank's performance in its first six years was far beyond expectations. By 1996, the bank became publicly quoted, and the opening share price was ₦8—eight times the share value when I invested six years earlier. The return on equity was any investor's dream. The share price had grown significantly, and the units held by me also increased due to bonus issues. I had earned multiples of dividends and bonuses besides my basic salary, allowances, and profit share. As a shareholder, I was enjoying dividends and bonus issues. At the same time, as an employee, I was benefitting from employee bonuses and dividends from employee share option. Within six years, my investment had yielded returns beyond my wildest imagination. My investment made me a multimillionaire. In the intervening years, I built my personal house and other investments globally, which was financed from income generated from my investments.

As is the case with successful entrepreneurship, investing requires passion, commitment, and patience. Investing is not a venture to be entered into frivolously; it is serious business and must be pursued with total commitment and focus. You must have the desire and determination to lift yourself out of poverty and create wealth.

The reality is that investing requires funds. You need money to invest, and the easiest source is from accumulated savings, unless of course, you have inherited money or won the lottery. The attitude of most people to investing is similar to their mind-set on saving. Why should I invest when I am struggling financially? How do I get the initial cash to invest in shares and stocks? Is there a risk I can lose it all?

From a survey of five hundred Nigerians with a monthly income ranging from ₦50,000 to ₦500,000, 72 percent own no investment instrument, while 28 percent own investments in one of, or a combination of, real estate (mostly personal homes), publicly quoted equities, and private business or private equity. The majority, who had no form of investment, gave various reasons for their inability to save or invest: "I can hardly survive on my salary, I simply have nothing left to save or invest"; "Only wealthy people can afford to invest"; "I don't understand the stock market; it's too risky and sophisticated"; "I know it is good to save, but I am not ready for it until I build or buy a home."

A simultaneous survey of five hundred wealthy Nigerians showed that 92 percent owned at least one business enterprise and owned investments in equities and real estate. Remarkably, 65 percent of the respondents described their childhood as impoverished. They built up their wealth through years of entrepreneurship and investing. Fifty-eight percent of the respondents started their business enterprise with their savings and funds borrowed from family and friends. Sixty percent of the respondents admitted struggling before their businesses took off.

This simply means that there is no economic situation that should deter anyone from investing. In truth, investing is much easier for entrepreneurs who earn a good income and who are willing to diversify to improve their earning potential. This is particularly true if they are adept at managing their personal finances and can set aside a part of their income regularly. It is important to have a basic knowledge of the various products available and stay updated on financial news. The best investors should engage professionals like stockbrokers, investment advisers, tax experts, and legal experts to maximize the benefits derivable from the various instruments.

In more developed economies, more reliable investment options are available. These markets are more transparent and better regulated. For the most part, the investing public is confident about the reliability of information emanating from these markets. In contrast, investment options are relatively limited in developing or emerging markets. These markets are less transparent and more susceptible to external and internal shocks.

Financial and real assets include private equity in businesses, publicly quoted equities, government securities, bonds, derivatives, convertibles, foreign currency denominated instruments, currency trading, unit trusts, and real estate. These investment instruments are available to everybody in any part of the world. The benefits derived from these investments are called returns. The return on private and publicly quoted equities is called dividend; the return on corporate and municipal bonds is called interest; and that on real estate is known as rental income. When these investments are sold, there might be gains or losses. The gains are called capital gains, and the losses are simply losses. Investing comes with the risk of not getting any returns, or even the loss of the capital invested. For example, it is possible to buy shares worth ₦5 million and not receive any dividend for years. It is also possible that the market value of the shares will be zero or completely worthless after several years.

These are the potential risks of investing. Investment decisions can be complex and require detailed knowledge and expert advice. The most prolific investors use experts and advisers in making vital decisions. A robust understanding of the workings of the money and capital markets will enable you to get the best out of the myriad of wealth instruments available to a potential investor.

The courage and willingness to take on calculated risks in order to achieve a major business breakthrough is what defines the most successful investors. The surest way to significant wealth creation is the combination of owning a successful business enterprise and substantial interest in equities/wealth instruments, including real estate.

My first education on investing came from my older cousin. By the time I returned from studying in the United States and started my career at the Central Bank of Nigeria, he was already a senior manager at a reputable oil and gas company. He lived in Port Harcourt at the time, so he periodically asked me to collect his dividend warrants on his behalf and deposit them into his account in Lagos. Out of curiosity, I inquired about his interest in equities. To my surprise, he showed me an Excel spreadsheet with his equities in several blue chip companies. I was thoroughly impressed but felt I was not yet in a financial position to spend "free money" on shares.

One afternoon in 1984, I decided to become an active investor. I was twenty-nine years old at the time. I approached my bank manager about acquiring a loan. In addition to direct deduction from my salary, he explained that he also needed collateral to secure the loan. He gave me a list of items I could use as collateral—real estate, quoted shares, and a third-party guarantee from anyone with real estate or quoted shares.

Clearly, I was unable to secure the loan at the time, as the conditions were too stringent for me. Instead, I decided to start investing in stocks. I opened an account with a stock broking firm down the street from my office and started buying quoted equities. From that point onward, I consistently set aside 10 percent of my monthly salary and sent it to my broker, giving him the latitude to buy any stock on my behalf. In my latter years, I developed a habit of recycling dividends and any windfall income from bonus and profit shares back to my broker to buy more shares. I began to follow the stock market closely and read up on news reports that could affect my investments. By the time I became sold on buying equities, no day went by without me having a conversation with my broker about the hottest stocks. I received periodic advice from the broker. Playing in the stock market became a hobby for me.

One day, I received a profit bonus from my bank and considered spending it on a trip to Spain. I had a conversation with my broker, who recommended I buy more Nestlé shares because he felt its price was bound to rise. I trusted his judgment and cancelled my proposed trip. I sent him a check to buy the shares. It was a wise decision, because

Nestlé's share price rose, as he had predicted. I made a handsome profit when I eventually sold off the shares.

The most common form of investing is trading in quoted equities or shares listed on the stock exchange. There are also fixed-interest and low-risk instruments like, bonds, convertibles, and certificates of deposit. You can also invest in mutual funds or unit trusts, where you buy units in a company, which are then invested in baskets filled with different types of stocks. There are also specialized funds like real estate investment trusts (REITs), international equity funds, and emerging market equity funds. Lately, there has been an explosion in cryptocurrency investments, as well as specialized or target funds. Potential investors need not be confused by the array of products and their accompanying technical jargon, but it is imperative to develop investment habits.

Investing in Private Enterprise

This form of investing is riskier and less regulated than publicly quoted equities. It has a greater potential for wealth creation if you bet correctly. Determined entrepreneurs have great ideas and creative products but need investors who believe in them to come on board and share the risk and reward. They recognize that they may have great ideas or products, but they need partners with expertise or funds.

Private equity firms are investment management companies who pool funds from individual investors, pension funds, and other sources to make investments in start-up companies and small businesses that show potential for growth. This is often called venture capital. These firms serve as advisers and conduits for investors who have a strong appetite for risk and who wish to create or grow their wealth. Some of these firms specialize in matchmaking potential investors with start-ups who have great potential but lack the needed capital. Many global technology giants were formed through this financing method, and a good number of investors have reaped great returns from their investment.

It is a riskier form of investment because of a reliance on the competence and track record of the private equity firm advising on a new venture investment. The investment document will state the minimum amount to expected be invested, the price per unit, the financial projection, and the expected rate of return over a stated period. The risk of loss of capital is high, so the expected return on investment is usually much higher than in publicly quoted equities.

There have been recorded cases of fantastic returns in private equity investment. A recent example is Facebook's $19 billion acquisition of WhatsApp—the largest ever private acquisition of a venture-capital-backed company. WhatsApp was initially funded with venture capital through a private equity firm. The initial investment of $60 million by Sequoia Capital was eventually valued at $3 billion at acquisition. Similarly, successful internet-based companies like Facebook, Groupon, Google, Airbnb, and LinkedIn sourced for their initial funding through private equity firms, and the investors reaped bountiful returns when the companies went public.

Investing in Publicly Quoted Equities

Investing in publicly quoted equities is the most popular form of investment. The markets can be traded globally and are easy to join and exit. They are transparent and well regulated and can be managed real time from anywhere in the world. You may live in Nigeria and invest in the Hong Kong Stock Exchange without setting foot in Hong Kong. This is a classic example of the universality of wealth creation.

The most common myth about investing in equities is that it is very risky. Equity investment is much safer than many other forms of investing. What is often lacking is adequate knowledge and understanding of the dynamics of the stock market. Legendary investor Warren Buffett once said, "Risk comes from not knowing what you're doing."

To understand the workings of the stock market, you have to acquire knowledge by reading voraciously and consistently tracking news about it. Understanding the market is the key to spotting opportunities and avoiding unnecessary risks. If you are investing in equities, it is advisable to operate an investment account with a stockbroker and discuss long-term investment objectives, which for a young person should be capital growth, safety, and income, in that order. For a young person hoping to create wealth, investing in equities is a long-term game. Nobel Prize–winning economist Paul Samuelson remarked, "Investing should be more like watching paint dry or watching grass grow. If you want excitement, take $800 and go to Las Vegas."

Starting early has advantages, because your investment account will grow as you grow older. A decade of investment usually is the expected threshold to see healthy returns, so the earlier you start, the better for your pockets. Investing can be fun, addictive, and ultimately rewarding, which is contrary to the more popular notions of it being very risky.

Investing in quoted equities will come in handy whenever you are prepared to start a business, acquire an existing venture, or invest in private equity. Without your own contribution or your savings, you will find it difficult to attract outside sources of funding. Your savings send a clear message to would-be investors and partners that you are disciplined, focused, tenacious, and ready to risk your own money before theirs.

Investing in Real Estate

In 2001, I came across a real estate investment opportunity that I could not undertake alone but that I thought could be a real winner. I consequently formed a consortium with four of my friends so we could mount a competitive bid for the acquisition of Ikoyi Hotels. At the time, it was a run-down and abandoned hotel owned by the federal government, yet it was located in the center of a high-brow area of Lagos. It had been earmarked for privatization, and the government had hoped to sell it to the highest bidder. We won the bid at the steep price of $13.8 million. We were faced with the challenge of raising that amount of money within a stipulated time frame. We decided to take in more investors: the original promoters held on to 51 percent, while 49 percent was shared among the other investors. I was able to pay for my units by selling off some equities and leveraging some debt. What had initially seemed an impossible investment was now part of my investment portfolio. The hotel was rebuilt and relaunched under the brand name Southern Sun, Ikoyi and managed by the Southern Sun Hotel Group of South Africa. As a result of all the changes, the real estate value of the hotel skyrocketed. Years later, the proceeds of a single round of equity sale were a hundred times more valuable than my initial investment.

Real estate investment is the business of buying, developing, and selling real estate assets for profit. There are three key elements in this definition: acquiring, developing, and selling.

- *Acquiring real estate assets.* This includes virgin land, homes, commercial property, abandoned and dilapidated property, foreclosed property, farmland, waterlogged land, reclaimed, and swampy land.
- *Developing real estate assets.* You may wish to develop the real estate into something more marketable that can attract higher returns. This means that you are adding value to it, either by building a new structure on it, remodeling an existing one, or converting from one use to another.
- *Selling real estate assets.* This involves selling or leasing out the real estate and converting your assets into cash and profit.

Many people get involved in real estate primarily for sentimental reasons, the thought of it as an investment usually being secondary. In virtually every part of Nigeria, owning a home is the ultimate measure of success. Most people feel unfulfilled until they build or acquire a home. It is more common to view real estate as a status symbol than as an instrument of wealth creation; consequently, many people get into unnecessary debt or even bankrupt themselves simply to own a home. Most people struggle to build or buy a home yet remain unable to create wealth.

Some people use their lifetime savings to acquire a home due to the difficulties faced in mortgage financing, as well as high interest rates. When they are able to secure some form of mortgage facility, they spend the rest of their lives servicing these loans. This puts a strain on their finances and plunges them deeper into the poverty trap. To compound their predicament, they hold on to these assets even when they appreciate or depreciate in value. They are unable to refinance, thus transferring the asset (or liability) to their offspring.

Investing in real estate can be a ticket out of poverty. Real estate should be seen as a form of investment and an instrument of wealth creation, not a mere status symbol. The following is a guide for people interested in creating wealth through real estate:

- Develop a passion for real estate and start dreaming and thinking about it.
- Get an education in any related discipline—business administration, economics, accounting, law, engineering, building technology, estate management, or surveying.
- Consistently pursue information about the real estate market around you and in other parts of the world.
- Identify any successful real estate entrepreneur and choose him or her as your mentor. If you can, get a job or an internship in a real estate firm for a firsthand knowledge of the business.
- Start saving at an early age. Discipline is key.
- When you know you are ready—preferably a few years after graduation or of working in a real estate establishment—partner with someone who shares your passion for the business to establish a limited liability company. Strategic partnerships make the process a lot less burdensome. In addition, partnering with people with other competencies and experiences can be a big advantage to the success of your organization.
- Think big but start small. Draw up a detailed business plan and ensure you implement the plan faithfully. Pick your first project carefully and put all your effort into making it a success. The success of your first project is key to building confidence, momentum, and a track record for future projects.

Your first project may be as small as acquiring a low-cost flat sold by the government in a new housing estate or buying a plot of land in a remote part of town and building a bungalow on it. You can raise the capital by dipping into your savings and borrowing at low interest from friends and family members. Avoid expensive loans at all cost. *Do not live in this property.* If you are presently living in a rented place, stay there. See the new property strictly as an investment. Your strategy should be to either lease it or sell it outright for a profit. As long as the rate of return is higher than the interest rate and rate of inflation, you are covered.

Once you have successfully concluded your first transaction, it becomes easier to execute the next one. Each successful project further solidifies your experience and boosts your confidence. Next, begin to strategize on the next property to acquire and keep challenging yourself by looking out for bigger opportunities. Dream big! It is only by aiming high that you attain great heights. Never feel intimidated or overwhelmed.

Successfully investing in real estate requires a thorough understanding of the business of property management, the investment climate, and the financial market. You also have to be passionate about it. A real estate entrepreneur is a calculated risk-taker who is courageous and determined. One of the attractions of investing in real estate is that the turnaround time is usually shorter, and the rate of return is relatively higher than investment in a business enterprise.

"Rule 72" is a rule that will guide you regarding the profitability of any investment but is relevant to real estate investments in particular. The rule states that dividing seventy-two by the rate of return on any investment will give you the number of years it will take to double the principal on the investment.

For instance, if an investment has an annual return of 6 percent simply divide seventy-two by six to find out how long it would take to double your principal. In this case, it will take twelve years to double your principal in an investment that yields 6 percent per annum. If the rate of return is 12 percent, it will take six years to double your principal. Therefore, if you invest $1 million in an asset that yields an annual rate of return of 12 percent, you should expect to have an asset worth at least $2 million in six years, all things being equal.

Take, for example, the hypothetical acquisition of a hundred-unit apartment complex in a high-profile neighborhood, which costs $10 million. Assuming you need an additional $2 million for renovation, repairs, permits, approvals, and other associated closing costs, the total investment is approximately $12 million. The estimated period of renovation is six months; projected period of sale, another six months— meaning twelve months to complete the project and sell all the units.

The entrepreneur can explore several funding options to raise the required $12 million. He or she might start with a personal contribution by teaming up with others to raise a significant part of the total required. The entrepreneur could approach interested investors, banks, and other financiers, who will earn a substantial 67 percent annual rate of return on a twelve-month investment. (It is not unusual for prospective buyers to wholly finance a project if it is considered "hot" and confidence in the promoter is strong. This is called spontaneous financing, a process very common with banks.) If each unit is sold for $220,000, the revenue generated will be $10 million. 8/12 x 100 percent = 67 percent. Using Rule 72, the period it takes to double the principal is 72/67 = 1.07 years.

The above example may seem unusually profitable but is typical of a number of real estate transactions, particularly if it is well thought out and handled by experienced professionals who have a successful track record.

While investing in real estate seems like a sure way to wealth creation, it is not entirely risk-free or rosy. Most real estate investment failures arise due to external factors like a sudden and unexpected change in government policy, a sudden increase in borrowing cost, unanticipated economic recession, or a mismatch of tenor, interest rate, and rate of return.

I have been privileged to observe one of Nigeria's most successful real estate investors—Otunba Subomi Balogun. I learned a lot watching him manage and expand his vast real estate portfolio. His most significant and strategic real estate investment was the acquisition of the prime property located at 19 Tinubu Street, Lagos, which for many years was the corporate headquarters of his bank.

According to Otunba Subomi Balogun in his memoir, *The Cross, The Triumph and The Crown*: "My top priority was to develop a corporate headquarters for my business and this materialised when I was informed by a good friend, Allan Shelley, Managing Partner at Knight, Frank & Rutley, Estate Managers, that a site owned and formerly occupied by the oldest British Pharmaceutical company in Nigeria, May & Baker Limited, and which was also originally the site of the first Italian Consulate in Nigeria, was available for sale with an approved building plan for eight floors ... The asking price was ₦1.5 million."

This was in 1979—a year after he resigned his appointment to set up his own company, City Securities—and he was already dreaming of building the headquarters of his business! Number 19 Tinubu Street— located in the heart of Lagos Island and next door to the Central bank of Nigeria and the Nigerian Stock Exchange buildings—was prime property. Balogun was determined to buy the property, and he won the bid, edging out a larger competitor, Bank of America (which later became Savannah Bank). The corporate headquarters was constructed over the next year, and the building was christened Primrose Tower. The dedication plaque wording, written by him, reads as follows:

> The Block "Primrose Tower" is dedicated to the Glory of God, as an embodiment of a young man's faith in the unfailing support of the Almighty God and his own Destiny, in spite of the seemingly insurmountable obstacles. It is also a monument of a young Nigerian's determination to succeed and to prove that, given the opportunity, he has the mettle to attain the commanding heights in the management of a financial institution. It serves as a lesson to all mankind that in all things, mortal men may have their say, but in the final analysis, the Almighty God will have His way.

This statement aptly captured the vision, sacrifice, and determination of the young entrepreneur. A less ambitious person would have been intimated by the status of the cobidder and its financial implication. Balogun took up the challenge, realizing that the property was a major step toward achieving his dream of owning a bank. Ownership of the property was part of his application for a banking license, and it assured the authorities of Balogun's seriousness and capability. He later created Primrose Properties Development Company to manage his vast real estate investments, and today, the company is worth its weight in gold, simply due to his foresight, vision, zeal, and determination.

CHAPTER 8

Lessons in Leadership

From the Corporate Boardroom to the Political Arena

Everything rises and falls on leadership.
　　　　　　　　　　　　—John C. Maxwell

If your actions inspire others to dream more, learn
more, do more and become more, you are a leader.
　　　　　　　　　　　　—John Quincy Adams

One of the most important elements of wealth creation in any society
is good leadership. Good leaders bring the best out of people; they
motivate others to do great things. One-time American secretary of
state Henry Kissinger observed, "The task of the leader is to get their
people from where they are to where they have not been." Leaders
strive to create an environment where citizens or subordinates can
flourish. Leaders instill in their people a hope for success and a belief
in themselves.

　It goes without saying that all wealthy and successful people are
natural leaders. Indeed, the rules of wealth are synonymous with the
characteristics of good leadership. You cannot attain the status of a

wealthy person if you do not imbibe the qualities of a good leader. Good leadership cuts across all aspects of life; family, community, corporate, and political leadership share the same fundamental elements. Positive leaders empower people to accomplish their goals. This is as relevant to business leadership as it is to political leadership.

Over the course of my life, I have been privileged to have worked directly with four exceptional leaders. Each one has been a mentor to me at one point or another, and they have played instrumental roles in my career and journey in life. It was through Otunba Balogun that I got my first introduction to the world of entrepreneurship and a culture of excellence in the workplace. Tayo Aderinokun and Fola Adeola instilled in me discipline, integrity, vision and focus, transparency, resilience, and doggedness. And then there is Asiwaju Bola Ahmed Tinubu.

December 2002 marked the beginning of my fifth year as MD/CEO of First Atlantic Bank. We had just completed what I considered a very successful financial year: our profits grew significantly, and the bank had successfully concluded its first year as a quoted stock on the floor of the Nigerian Stock Exchange. One evening, I was seated behind my desk, looking forward to the coming year with excitement and confidence, when my phone rang. It was Tokunbo Afikuyomi, the senator representing Lagos Central.

Sounding businesslike, he told me that Asiwaju Bola Ahmed Tinubu—at the time the executive governor of Lagos State—wanted to have a meeting with me urgently. I barely knew the governor and was surprised by the invitation, so I asked the senator what the meeting was about. He refused to divulge the purpose, saying that I would find out when I met the governor.

That meeting was the beginning of the extraordinary events that catapulted me to the position of the deputy governor of Lagos State. The decision to have me as his deputy was entirely his own. I was delighted to be given the rare opportunity to serve Lagos State. As I would come to understand, Asiwaju Tinubu trusts his own instinct and makes his judgment about people by a careful study of their character and pedigree.

Asiwaju Bola Tinubuis is widely regarded as a political colossus, but unknown to most people is his business acumen. Through a combination of solid entrepreneurial skills, dexterity in financial management, and a populist approach to governance, he has been able to make a significant impact in the lives of millions of people. He trained as an accountant and worked with several multinationals, including Arthur Andersen; Deloitte, Haskins, and Sells; and Mobil Producing Nigeria. He was successful in the world of business before emerging as a political leader. He has deftly applied his entrepreneurial skills—honed during his years in the corporate world—to great effect in the political terrain.

When he was elected governor in 1999, he met the state's finances in a mess: there were problems in revenue generation, education, health care, the environment, transportation, and the public service. To tackle these challenges, Asiwaju Tinubu assembled a team comprised of competent and talented technocrats and politicians. Together, they crafted a twenty-four-year development blueprint for the transformation of the state.

Over the next few years, Asiwaju Tinubu and his team worked tirelessly to transform and modernize the state, while improving the living standard of the people of Lagos State. He introduced new initiatives such as the Private Sector Participation (PSP) in waste management, the Lagos Area Metropolitan Transportation Authority (LAMATA), and the Bus Rapid Transit (BRT) system to tackle challenges in the transportation sector.

I was excited about the opportunity to serve as deputy governor in 2003, but I was also conflicted because I was leaving my comfortable position at First Atlantic—a bank in which I owned a 15 percent stake— for the sensitive and exalted office of deputy governor. This was way out of my comfort zone. I had neither been a politician nor held any public office at the time, and I was unsure of how things would turn out. My anxieties quickly disappeared once I was sworn in, because the governor created a working environment that made me feel comfortable serving alongside him. He gave me a free hand in setting up my office and my team and entrusted me with responsibilities that were consequential to the transformation plan.

Some of my appointees included the head of investment banking at First Atlantic, Babajide Sanwo-Olu; my head of corporate affairs at First Atlantic, Dayo Yemi-Lawal; and Henry Balogun, a brilliant lawyer who became my chief of staff. In addition, the governor seconded Barrister (now Senator) Opeyemi Bamidele as my political adviser. Within a few days, my team was in place.

My first major assignment as deputy governor was to head the committee in charge of rejuvenating the internally generated revenue of the state. Through Asiwaju Tinubu's support and exceptional leadership, the committee was able to overhaul the state's revenue generation system, which in turn led to an exponential increase in the state's income. The blueprint created by the committee would later be adopted by the Federal Inland Revenue Service (FIRS) and by several states in the country.

Asiwaju Tinubu was the first governor in Nigeria to fully adopt and implement private-public partnership in governance. He was a visionary who saw the potential of the collaboration between government and the organized private sector to bring about solutions to many public sector challenges. For instance, in 2000, he attempted to solve the perennial problem of power outages through a strategic partnership with the private sector. American energy conglomerate, Enron, was interested in disposing its floating barges. Asiwaju Tinubu immediately assembled a negotiating team, and the barges were acquired and installed at Egbin Power Station, near Ikorodu, Lagos State. Today, Egbin Power Station is the largest power-generating station in Nigeria. The inflexibility of the federal government made it impossible for the state government to be the sole beneficiary of the initiative, but Asiwaju's doggedness in relation to the power station has been beneficial to the entire country.

Before his tenure as governor, the federal and state government had unsuccessfully combated the perennial flooding of Victoria Island by the Atlantic Ocean. Upon resumption of office, he approached the problem from an entrepreneurial viewpoint. He invited the private sector to study the problem, which eventually resulted in the partnership with Energyx Group to turn what was a flood-prone beachfront to Africa's largest new city—the Eko Atlantic City. The new city is expected to accommodate more than 250,000 residents and commuters.

Asiwaju Tinubu's transformational blueprint was also impactful on the education landscape, where he embarked on a major renovation of school buildings and infrastructure across the state. He also started the payment of WAEC examination fees to alleviate the hardship of parents who struggled to pay. This practice soon became the standard nationwide, as other governors soon emulated the gesture. The governor also transformed the transportation system of the state when he created the LAGBUS and introduced the Bus Rapid Transit (BRT) system. He reconstructed major roads in the state—particularly in the central business districts of Lagos Island, Ikoyi, Victoria Island, Surulere, Ikeja, Mushin, Oshodi, and Ikorodu, as well as other parts of Lagos.

Governor Tinubu's giant strides quickly became the benchmark for other states and the foundation upon which future governors in Lagos have built upon. His unrivalled understanding of the political terrain and his ability to win the heart of the electorate during electioneering made a profound impression on everyone. We won the election for a second term in April 2003. It was a keenly contested election, as all other AD governors in the Southwest lost to the PDP.

As we settled into our second term, I became more engrossed with the job. With time, the governor was no longer just my boss but also my friend and mentor. I began to study his political and administrative style more closely. I gladly accepted the assignments and responsibilities he gave me, which further broadened my knowledge of the job. In turn, he rewarded me with more responsibilities.

The next three years were as exciting as they were challenging. We faced a relentless onslaught from the PDP-controlled federal government, whose leaders piled political and economic pressure on the governor and the state. The governor was determined to succeed, and he survived all the missiles thrown at him. He remained resolute and focused on his goals, particularly during the period when the federal government illegally withheld the state's local government allocation in a desperate bid to weaken the governor politically. It was a trying period, but the governor had assembled a solid team of seasoned politicians and legal and financial experts, and we were able to collectively weather the storm.

Over the course of my career, I have seen how great leadership can make a significant difference to the fortunes of an organization. The same applies to societies and nations. One of the most inspirational stories of national transformation in recent times is that of Singapore, which is captured in the book *From Third World to First*. Its story illustrates how leadership can transform a nation culturally and economically. A few decades ago, Singapore, like most African nations, was a third world country. But it lifted itself out of the doldrums and is now one of the most prosperous countries in the world. Lee Kuan Yew, the leader most responsible for this transformation, once noted, "A nation is great not by its size alone. It is the will, the cohesion, the stamina, the discipline of its people and the quality of their leaders which ensure it an honourable place in history."

I learned the most difficult lessons in leadership during the years I served as deputy governor of Lagos State, particularly during the period of electioneering and politicking. By the final year of our second term, I felt I was ready to take up a higher responsibility. I believed that I had discharged my duties to the best of my abilities, and I was hopeful that I would emerge as the party's governorship candidate. I was ready to succeed my boss as governor.

As is always the case in the context of succession politics, there was palpable tension within the rank of the party. Some of the other aspirants who had also shown interest include Ganiyu Solomon, Remi Adikwu-Bakare, Adekunle Lawal, Rahmon Owokoniran, Omotilewa Aro-Lambo, Tokunbo Afikuyomi, Jimi Agbaje, and Hakeem Gbajabiamila.

In October 2006, I launched my campaign to be governor and was optimistic of my chances. Unfortunately, this was not meant to be. Babatunde Raji Fashola, a brilliant lawyer and chief of staff to the governor at the time, was nominated as the party's candidate, and the rest is history.

I am certain that Governor Tinubu chose his successor after torturous deliberations. It could not have been an easy task for him, and I do not envy the burden he must have shouldered at the time. In the heat of the political intrigues, I recall a private meeting between myself and the governor. The meeting was lengthy but very civil. The governor took his time to hear my grievances but made his decision clearly known to me.

In the immediate aftermath of the election, I found myself at a critical crossroads. At this particular juncture, I made no immediate plans to return to banking. I had detached myself from my primary banking constituency, as my main focus was governance and politics. With no fallback plan on hand and having lost the party's nomination, I had to reset my political and professional trajectory.

Almost six years later, I was opportune to meet privately with Asiwaju Tinubu again. I recounted our last meeting at his office. He spoke candidly and counselled me against quitting active politics. He believed I still had a lot to contribute to the party and the nation. It was all the motivation I needed, and I have been able to serve in several capacities ever since.

I have recounted the circumstances surrounding the politics of succession in governance to emphasize the difficulties nations face in choosing its leaders. In this book, I have illustrated in great detail the story of many successful institutions and their core values. If a relatively unknown brand like Guaranty Trust Bank could, within thirty years, transform into arguably one of the most successful banks in Africa and beyond, then a country like Nigeria can be transformed if it adopts the same qualities and values highlighted in this book. For our nation to excel, transformative leadership, reformative leadership, transparent leadership, and courageous leadership are critical ingredients of the type of political leadership required.

One of the key fundamentals of any successful businesses is that the owners (leaders) have manifested the rules of wealth as enunciated in this book and have created wealth in the process. Likewise, the nation needs these types of leaders to transform Nigeria into a wealthy nation. For this reason, my belief is that leadership in the corporate environment can be used to transform a nation.

CHAPTER 9

EPILOGUE: Climbing the Ladder

Shortly before the publication of this book, the COVID-19 pandemic popularly known as the "Corona Virus" paralyzed the world. The outbreak reportedly started around the Wuhan province in China towards the end of 2019, and quickly spread to every corner of the globe. The pandemic left in its wake, millions of infected people and thousands of deaths globally. In addition, the virus caused severe economic distress to the world economy, nations, communities, businesses and individuals of all classes.

The news emanating from China in relation to the virus was scanty at the onset, as the general impression was that the Chinese authorities had effectively contained the virus and prevented a worldwide spread. As days went by, it became obvious that the virus was deadlier than initially reported and had spread wider than initially thought. As fatalities grew in China and across the globe, the World Health Organization proclaimed it a pandemic on March 11, 2020. The virus became the catalyst for a global recession that would eventually take months -if not years- for many businesses and individuals to recover.

At the height of the outbreak, the world economy fell into recession.

Most economies either completely shut down or operated at very low capacity. Major world economic indicators declined significantly. There was so much uncertainty and volatility, to the extent that oil prices, stock prices, currencies, international trade, interest rates and bond rates all showed significant and consistent decline in value.

A global pandemic of this nature is no respecter of persons, class, race or geography. . In many ways, it acted as a global leveler, and reminded everyone of how vulnerable our lives- and indeed our pockets- truly are. Nevertheless, it dawned on me that the antidote for the economic poison of viruses like COVID-19 is the Formula for Wealth as highlighted in this book.

I knew there would be severe economic consequences once the COVID-19 crisis became public knowledge. The alarm bells started ringing for me in January 2020, when China decided to close factories, ban travel and quarantine millions of people. China is a major exporter of consumer, intermediate and capital goods all over the world, and I suspected that shortages would start to show up in stores and markets, thereby precipitating price uncertainty and instability. The situation abruptly escalated in February, when other countries began to impose travel bans. The global stock markets became highly volatile and currencies became unstable. By March 2020, the stock market index and many national currencies had lost substantial value.

The real test of a person's financial security comes at the onset of a global pandemic or an economic crisis. In many parts of the world, the shut-down meant that economic activities grounded to a halt, which exposed the fragility of the system and the people. Hourly and daily-paid employees, self -employed persons and most small and medium-sized businesses and their employees had no immediate source of income. It became evident fairly quickly that a lot of people generally do not have sufficient enough savings to cushion the immediate impact of a crisis of this magnitude. Most people were instantly thrown into financial anguish, and the cries of a government bail-out reverberated across the land.

The truth is most people that fall under this category have always been stuck in poverty trap (as discussed in Chapter 3-The True Face of Poverty). The economic storm caused by COVID-19 was all it took to expose the true financial condition of many people. The fortunate few that had already attained financial security prior to the outbreak were able to tap into their financial assets to sustain themselves. The immediate impact of the COVID-19 economic crisis was that it separated those with financial security from those within the poverty trap. People that were heavily dependent on their monthly salary and without accumulated savings, as well as people with poorly capitalized micro-businesses, suffered during the period. Many were affected by the economic recession, because they became jobless with no means of regular income and were at the bottom of the food chain with little or no protection from the economic fall-out.

This book provides the way out for everyone in the poverty trap whether or not they are aware that they are indeed in the trap. The Formula for Wealth is the antidote for economic difficulties, provided you are willing to imbibe the foundational principles in Chapter 5 (The Rules of Wealth) and the fundamental principles in Chapters 6 and 7 (Fundamentals of Entrepreneurship and Money Earns Money).

The process of climbing out of the poverty trap into financial security is better demonstrated with what I call the 'Climbing the Ladder' concept. This is the methodical approach to wealth creation that adopts the global concepts of the rules of wealth and the fundamental principles that have been tested over time. This process is time-consuming, and requires patience, commitment, courage, perseverance, doggedness and determination. Unless you are able to muster these attributes- and faithfully adopt the rules and fundamentals in the formula for wealth- you may remain trapped in poverty for a long time.

Everyone on the journey to ultimate wealth is climbing the proverbial wealth ladder. The ultimate goal is to reach the top of the ladder, which at the very least, fetches some form of financial security. Crises like COVID-19 are storms we face when climbing this ladder. The natural reaction for most people is to feel overwhelmed in the midst of a raging storm. The easiest thing to do is to abandon the journey due to the unexpectedness of the storm. However, anyone (with an intrinsic knowledge of the formula for wealth) that remains committed to get to the top will continue with their climb, irrespective of the circumstances.

If you are committed to wealth creation, remember the rules of wealth in Chapter 5. Rather than being overwhelmed by everything negative going on around you, imbibe a positive personal financial mindset. This is the time to possibly start afresh and rejuvenate oneself. New opportunities always open up in the midst of a crisis, and people with a positive mindset are better positioned to identify these opportunities. This book provides you with all the support you need to succeed. I implore you to revisit the previous chapters and digest its contents thoroughly.

Micro and small businesses are not immune to the shock that arises in the midst of a major economic crisis. In truth, micro businesses, sole proprietorships and one-man outfits face difficulties because they lack the knowledge of the fundamentals of entrepreneurship as highlighted in Chapter 6. Many of them are poorly capitalized with weak management and financial structures. They do not have business plans, viable budgets and financial statements. For businesses under this category, the simple rules of wealth highlighted in chapters 6 and 7 are essential. In the midst of an economic storm, these businesses are confronted by loss of opportunities, unpaid rent, unpaid interest and principal payments, and possibly the threat of bankruptcy. Under these circumstances, they will most certainly need help from the government and regulators to overcome some difficulties. It is however imperative for these businesses to help themselves by focusing primarily on low hanging fruits, and Chapter 5 of this book goes a long way towards helping business owners and entrepreneurs. These foundational principles are fundamental to successful entrepreneurship, are even more crucial during a period of economic stagnation or recession.

Successful entrepreneurs are not immune to the dangers that accompany the outbreak of a global pandemic or an economic crisis. These entrepreneurs have always done things right, and have religiously followed the rules of wealth. In the midst of a storm, it is important for these businesses to conduct a thorough review and diagnosis of the entire business- including its financial health, management and staffing, products and service review, sales and marketing, and finally, an industry and competition analysis. This will reveal the extent of the business' vulnerability, its strengths, weaknesses, potential threats and possible opportunities. For most businesses under this category, the primary protection during a recession is cash. Cash is king for businesses all the time, but particularly supreme for a business during periods of an economic slow-down. The key is to reduce cash outflows whilst attempting to increase cash inflows. Businesses must focus on generating net positive cash inflow consistently, at the expense of short term profits. For those who are able to navigate cash-flow problems with ease, Chapters 6 and 7 become essential reading, because periods of uncertainty almost always present a unique set of investment and expansion opportunities.

The wealthiest in society are not exempt from having to deal with the fallout of a global crisis. Chapter 2 of this book defines those who have attained the status of wealthy persons as those who not only have financial security, but also financial independence and quite possibly absolute financial freedom. In a period of economic uncertainty, their circumstances are unique and their challenges are different, but the impact fundamentally remains the same. Whenever economic activities, factories, offices, airports and borders are partially or wholly shut down, the outcome is that prominent industries including airlines, hotels, restaurants, tourism, sports, entertainments, oil and gas, construction, manufacturing and aviation enter a temporary coma. It is conceivable that the net worth of wealthy individuals shrinks in a recession. Indeed, the rich also cry. The wealthiest individuals are forced to scramble to protect their assets around the world. Businesses that have built successful enterprise and solid organizations feel the threat of overnight cracks in their empire. News headlines like: 'businesses closing down'; 'millions filing for unemployment benefits'; 'stock prices crashing'; 'threats of a banking collapse', amidst talk of 'currency devaluations' and 'civil unrest' send shivers to the spine of wealthy people. These situations- and circumstances- do not disappear overnight. In times of crises, there is no quick-fire remedy that can be applied.

This is comparable to a situation where a person at the top of the ladder suddenly finds himself in the midst of a storm. Crashing to the ground is not an option, because it is tantamount to total collapse and the death of the enterprise. The viable option is to hold on until the storm abates, or perhaps to climb to a lower level that could lighten the load. The wealthiest businesses survive these periods by quickly reorganizing, strategizing, refocusing and repositioning. Most well-structured businesses have the tools and resources to survive these storms over the long run.

Nation-states are not exempt from having to navigate the murky waters of a global crisis. The wealth of a nation is just as important as the wealth of its individuals and enterprise. Indeed, they are complementary and directly proportional. When a sizable number of individuals and enterprise within a nation are wealthy, the nation is wealthy. The 'climb the ladder' concept is just as relevant for nations. There are countries that are at the bottom of the ladder, some in the middle and a few at the top.

COVID-19 has exposed the fragility of the global economy. The most visible evidence was the collapse of oil prices. In a matter of weeks, the crude oil benchmark price crashed from around $65 per barrel to a staggering record low of under $17 per barrel. The decimation of the price of oil was caused in part by a disagreement between Russia and Saudi Arabia in relation to crude oil production outputs, as well as a global demand destruction resulting in the plummeting of production by virtually all major oil producers. The International Monetary Fund estimated that the world economy could shrink by more than 3% in 2020 and recovery might likely be prolonged. This is an extraordinary reversal from previous forecast of 3.3% growth for this year 2020 before the pandemic hit. The magnitude and speed of the collapse of the world economy is unprecedented which has inflicted untold damage to the economies of developed and developing countries.

This challenging period presents an acid test for every country's leadership. The measure of success would be determined by the quality and standard of leadership and the social capital that each nation had with its people, as well as the trust the people have in their leaders. A crisis requires strong, effective and positive leadership, and in the face of adversity, some leaders stepped up to the plate while others showed a lack of awareness and direction. The Formula for Wealth. If properly applied would go a long way towards building a new generation of business and political leaders to steer businesses and nations out of Great Depression into a prosperous future.

ABOUT THE AUTHOR

Femi Pedro

Femi Pedro is an economist, banker, entrepreneur, investor, and a political leader. He is also a mentor of young and aspiring entrepreneurs. He is currently chairman of the Small and Medium Enterprise Development Agency of Nigeria (SMEDAN) and the pioneer chairman of the Lagos State Sports Trust Fund (LSSTF).

Femi Pedro began his professional banking career at the Central Bank of Nigeria, before becoming one of the cofounders and seed investors at one of Africa's pioneer banks—Guaranty Trust Bank (GT Bank)—at the age of thirty-two. Within ten years, he became the managing director of First Atlantic Bank (FinBank) after acquiring the bank with a consortium of investors in 1998. He served as managing director of the bank until 2003, when he was elected to serve as the deputy governor of Lagos State—Nigeria's commercial capital and Africa's largest city-state.

In his years as the deputy governor of Lagos State, Femi Pedro worked alongside Governor Bola Tinubu to embark on an unprecedented and aggressive revenue drive by restructuring, reorganizing, and reengineering the entire revenue-generating mechanism of Lagos State. His wealth of experience in the banking sector as a leader, entrepreneur, and investor came to fruition as he copiloted the transformation of Lagos State. In his time in office, the foundation was laid for the ongoing economic evolution being witnessed in Lagos today.

Femi Pedro serves on the boards of various business ventures and has substantial investments in banking, real estate, information technology, manufacturing, and the hotel and hospitality sectors. An avid and passionate golfer, he is happily married to Honorable Justice Jumoke Pedro. Their union is blessed with children and grandchildren.